Programming from scratch

Gary Crandall

Follow the path from bits to apps

PSIpress

Perfectly Scientific Press
3754 SE Knight St.
Portland, OR 97202

First Perfectly Scientific Press paperback edition: December 2010.
Perfectly Scientific Press paperback ISBN: 978-1-935638-06-3

Cover concept by Naomi Borwein.

Cover design by Julia Canright.

Visit our website at www.perfscipress.com

Printed in the United States of America.
9 8 7 6 5 4 3 2 1 0

This book was printed on 15% post-consumer waste paper.

Preface

I've been developing software for over a quarter of a century. My journey over this terrain began as a hardware technician, some 35 years ago. I try to exploit my own history to advantage when instructing others on programming techniques.

I am somewhat amused when I observe a new generation of programmers requiring computer memory upgrades due to an "unworkable" environment of 1 gigabyte of RAM (essentially a billion bytes of memory storage). When I first started in this business, we had only 1 million bytes or even less. It is equally amusing now to watch 250 gigabytes of disk space rapidly filling to capacity, whereas in my youth, it might have taken two grown men to carry a 10-megabyte hard disk up the stairs.

Obviously, computer technology has advanced radically over the last 30 years, and I would never trade today's innovations for yesterday's archaic technology. But my point is that a new generation of developers has little or no understanding of what lies "under the hood," and, as a result, their excellence is limited. Quite literally, the abundance of technological innovation can *mask* a programmer's shortcomings.

One of the difficulties in learning how to program is that modern languages are at such a high level that they can render the student largely unaware of a computer's underlying structure. While such an understanding is not an absolute prerequisite to programming, a student should have at least some grasp of a computer's underlying structure in order to achieve optimal software results.

Hence, the journey to learn programming begins where it all started, many years ago. First, we shall walk through the evolution of software development, from the earliest computer concepts, to the most modern technology. Second, we will examine how to program slightly below the level that modern languages start, which is essential to understanding how higher level languages do what they do. And finally, we will explore the higher level languages used in the most recent devices, such as iPhones, web development, etc.

It is essential that you follow the material and exercises outlined in this book in the order they are given. You will acquire the greatest understanding by studying each section sequentially— without skipping over a seemingly boring or irrelevant section (unless the section specifically indicates that it is optional).

Key point: Wherever you see the "key" icon, there is a specific point being emphasized. These points will usually be a summary of the surrounding materials, and an important component to your learning.

Gary Crandall
Vancouver, WA
Dec 2010

Contents

Chapter 1:

Evolution of software

The most fundamental concept of computer technology is the base-2 numbering system, or *binary*. In fact, if it weren't for binary, it is unlikely that computers would have ever evolved.

To understand binary, let's first review some fundamentals about the numbering system you are probably the most familiar with—base-10. As we learned in early grade school, there are only 10 digits that make up our numbering system : 0, 1, 2, 3, 4, 5, 6, 7, 8, and 9. What this means is that any single digit of a multi-digit number can only be one of these 10 values.

Let's suppose we have a 3-digit timer that starts at zero, and that we increment the counter by 1, to obtain the following:

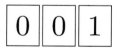

Now let's increment this timer by, say, 5, which would change the timer to 6:

Let's add 3 more, which will cause the timer to be 1 more increment away from overflowing to the next significant digit:

If we increment the timer one more time, by any value, the counter will increment the next digit to the left:

The fact that the timer overflows is obvious, but it is only obvious to us because we have grown accustom to the base-10 numbering system (all digits are represented by 0 through 9). But if we were to use a different numbering base, it might be difficult to adjust.

Base-2

Let's go through the same exercise as above, except this time, let's assume that each digit in our timer can only be one of two digits: either 0 or 1. In other words, a base-2 system:

So far, if we increment our base-2 timer by 1, it appears identical to the base-10 timer we are accustom to. However, if we increment the timer once more, the digit will overflow (since each digit can only contain 0 or 1):

Note that a base-2 readout of "010" is not a "ten," but rather, it is a value of *two*. We could add one more to obtain a value of "three" but it will look like this:

If we increment the base-2 timer once more, both digits will overflow to obtain this:

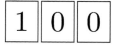

Again, a readout of "100" for base-2 is a value of "four" (not one hundred), because a counter will increment from 0 through 4 as 000, 001, 010, 011, and 100. Unless you are already familiar with binary, it might take a while to become accustomed to such a system. Yet, the native architecture of every computer, from inception until now, is binary.

Why binary?

Binary is the numbering system of choice for electronic technology, because base-2 is the essential anatomy of the most primitive electronic component of all: The switch.

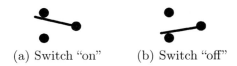

(a) Switch "on"   (b) Switch "off"

Figure 1.1: Switches represent binary because they have two states: "on" and "off."

In its simplest form, a switch has two positions: On or off, or one state versus another state. In binary terms, we could represent this with a "0" or "1." In the most primitive sense, we could use a series of simple electric switches to represent any binary number.

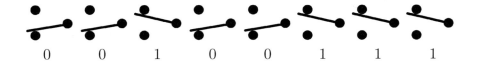

   0   0   1   0   0   1   1   1

Figure 1.2: A series of switches can represent a binary number.

If each switch in Figure 1.2 were representing a binary digit, then the whole series is representing the number "00100111," which happens to be the value thirty nine in base-10.

Using the switch example is not a mere analogy, but in fact, a reality. From the earliest computer to the most modern technology today, the anatomy of all data processing is the same: a giant array of switches. Of course, today's technology consists of electronic, microscopic switches, but the principle is the same.

The world of binary

Regardless of what a computer might appear to be, its native language is base-2, or binary. In fact, the only way to communicate

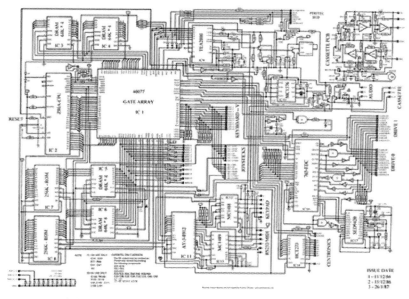

Figure 1.3: A "simple" data processing schematic with millions of electronic "switches."

to the earliest computers was through switch panels (such as the one shown in Figure 1.4), with indicators and switches that conveyed the literally binary computations occurring within the machine. As you can well imagine, this was a tedious, and even non-intuitive process.

It was immediately evident to the earliest engineers that a better communication system should be developed, and that led to the usage of *hexadecimal*, referring to base-16 arithmetic.

Base-16

So far, we have only discussed two numbering systems: Base-10, and base-2. In base-10, each digit of a number can be represented with one of ten values (0 through 9), while base-2's digits are

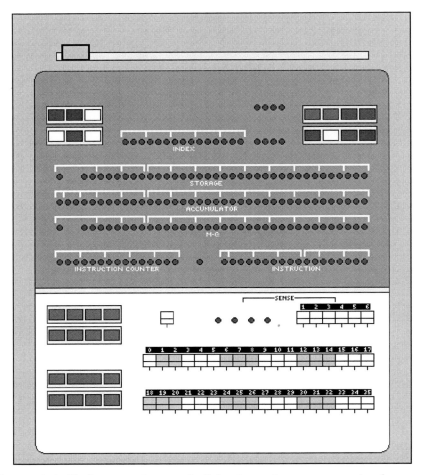

Figure 1.4: Early computer panel. Prior to modern programming language, computer instructions were literally entered as binary instructions using panels like this one.

represented by one of two values (0 or 1). A third method—which we are now introducing—is base-16, where any digit is represented by sixteen values: 0 through F.

In other words, if you were counting one by one, a hexadecimal digit would increment as 0, 1, 2, 3,...to 9, and then A, B, C, D, E, and F, for a total of 16 values before overflowing a digit.

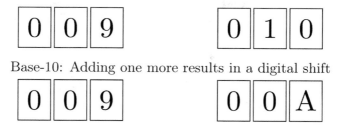

Base-10: Adding one more results in a digital shift

Hexadecimal: Adding one more increments to 'A' then 'B', etc.

Figure 1.5: The difference between base-16 and base-10.

Why hexadecimal?

Early computer pioneers began representing computer data with base-16 for two reasons. First, very large numbers could be represented with fewer digits than the native computer language of binary. Second, a base-16 numbering system is more intuitive to humans than base-2. And, at the same time, base-16 can easily represent an underlying binary value quite easily.

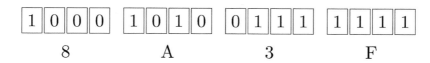

Figure 1.6: Hexidecimal can easily represent large binary numbers.

Consider the illustration in Figure 1.6. The top row is displaying a large number represented in binary, and the bottom row represents the same value, but in hexadecimal (base-16). Note that there is a one-for-one correspondence in value for every four binary digits, yet the hexadecimal representation requires far fewer physical digits.

Although hexadecimal representation was used extensively for the earliest development of computers, it is still used to this day to represent raw data elements in software. It is therefore to your advantage to become well versed in hexadecimal notation to enhance your programming skills.

 # Exercises

The following questions are designed to consult your understanding of this chapter. The correct answers can be found in the appendix.

1. What do a "switch" and a binary digit have in common?
2. What binary number will result if you add 1 to the binary value 011?
3. Write down the binary representation for the decimal value 9.
4. Given a hexadecimal value of 00FF, what hexadecimal value will result if you add 1?
5. Why is hexadecimal preferred over binary for representing a digital, computer number?

For further reading, explore the following website:

http://www.binarymath.info/

Chapter 2:

Anatomy of processing

We learned in the previous chapter that *binary* is the native "language" of a computer, and that binary values are best represented in base-16, or hexadecimal. But none of this explains how a computer operates or what makes it tick.

To fully understand how a computer functions, we will break it down into four general parts:

- Memory
- The processor
- The clock
- Peripherals

Memory

The term *memory* is interchangeable with *storage*. Computer memory, therefore, stores data and can be written or read at will.

No doubt, you have heard the term "RAM," "bytes," "gigabytes," etc., mentioned numerous times. "RAM" is an abbreviation for *random access memory*, which means that data can be stored and erased at arbitrary locations throughout the entire array of computer storage. A *byte* is an 8-digit binary value. Another name for a binary digit is bit, and hence, 8 bits constitute one byte.

A dollop of 1,024 bytes, or a *kilobyte*, is abbreviated with "K." A *megabyte*, roughly one million bytes (in modern terms 1,024 × 1,024 bytes), is abbreviated with "M" or *mega*. Exactly 1,024 mega, which is roughly one billion bytes, is abbreviated as "G" or "giga."

Hence, next time you hear a phrase like, "I have three gigabytes of RAM," you will know that it means "about 3 billion 8-bit values of random-access memory."

"Memory" within a computer is simply data storage. A conventional desktop or laptop computer typically contains several billion bytes of storage, and it is organized as a series of 32 or 64-bit values. Each of these values is identified by a *memory address*.

Each byte of storage has an associated, unique numerical address. A computer is able to access any one of its several billion bytes of storage through such addresses, and hence, the term *random access memory*, or RAM is derived.

The processor

The *processor* (also referred to as a microprocessor), stated simply, processes data. It is the "brains," if you will, of any computer.

Processors come in various sizes, and their usage ranges from simple household appliance managers to high-powered super computers. Regardless of their purpose or their power, they all function on the same principle: to execute instructions.

Figure 2.2 shows how the typical processor works. First, the processor fetches information from RAM, beginning at some predetermined memory address. The information it fetches will be a numerical "code" that instructs the processor to do something. What that *something* is depends on the code, but typical processor

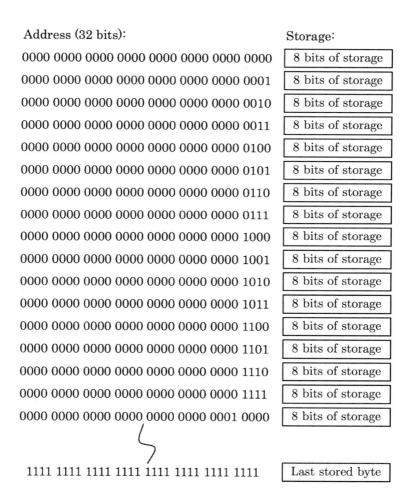

Figure 2.1: 32-bit memory architecture. Each byte of storage has an associated address. A computer is said to "randomly" access various memory locations through these addresses.

instructions are fairly low-level and mundane, such as "fetch the next four bytes which represent a memory address," or, "compare the next two bytes to the two bytes that follow." However, it is the series of such low-level instruction—perhaps hundreds of thousands of them—that eventually translate into sophisticated action.

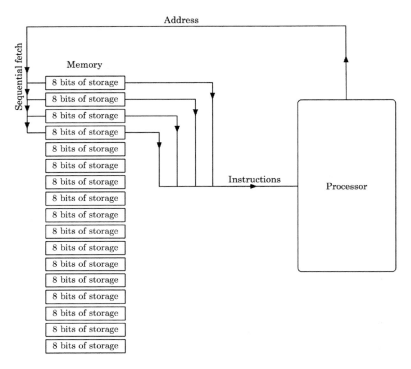

Figure 2.2: The cycle of a processor. The processor fetches information from sequential memory addresses, and each piece of information is a code that instructs the processor to do something.

Key point: Part of the lingo amongst programmers is the term *code*, as in, "I wrote some *code* today." The terms "code," "software," and "program" are often used interchangeably, but the origin of the word "code" is a numeric *code* that instructs the processor to execute.

The clock

All computers have a built-in clock. But by clock I do not mean a conventional timer with minutes and seconds. Rather, a computer clock runs at a very high rate of billions of cycles per second. The clock is the computer's heartbeat, which is what gives the processor "life."

In fact, it is the speed of the computer clock that determines the speed of execution, and this aspect is most noticeable in promotional material for various brands of processors. "New 6ghz processor!" The "processor" speed is really how fast the processor is driven by the clock signal.

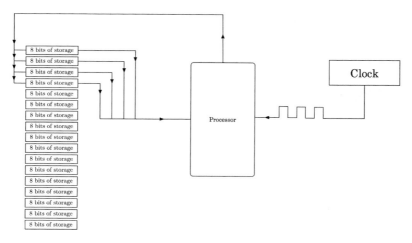

Figure 2.3: The "clock" is the electronic heartbeat that gives "life" to the processor.

The clock signal is what drives the processor, and this signal is literally the pulse that steps the processor through its tasks. One or more clock cycles cause the processor to fetch the next instruction from memory, the next few clock cycles march the processor through the execution of that instruction, the memory addresses are incremented, and the processing cycle repeats. This occurs hundreds of millions of times per second in the average computer.

Peripherals

A *peripheral* is a device that exists outside of the processor and outside of program memory. A peripheral can be a computer screen monitor, a keyboard, a mouse, or a hard disk drive. Generally, a peripheral is any device that communicates to and from the processor and the outside world.

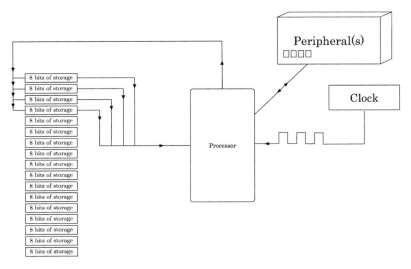

Figure 2.4: The processor sends and receives signals to and from outside peripherals. A peripheral can be a disk drive, a printer, a monitor, etc.

Peripherals are often defined as a computer's "input and output" architecture, or I/O for short. Essentially, anything that retrieves or receives information to and from the processor and its memory is considered part of the I/O system.

As a programmer, it is important to realize that your program is always executed in RAM memory, never from an outside peripheral. While a program can be *stored* on a peripheral, such as a hard disk drive, the program code must be first loaded into RAM memory in order for it to execute.

Programs send signals to peripherals and receive signals from peripherals, but an executing program always resides in RAM memory and can't be executed otherwise.

Where your program lives

If you create a software program, it eventually needs to reside in RAM memory in order for the program to run. Typically, the program codes are stored in a file on a disk drive, and the computer

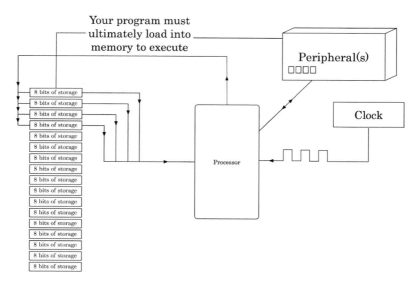

Figure 2.5: A program typically resides on a peripheral, such as a hard disk drive, but can only be executed from RAM memory.

must load it from the drive into its memory storage. Once loaded, the processor can execute the sequential codes.

The remainder of this book deals with the step-by-step process to create the programming codes that are first stored on the disk and then loaded into memory for the processor to execute.

 # Exercises

Given the two columns below, match each item in the left column with the appropriate description in the right column. For example, if two items on the left were "carrots" and "apples," and the two items on the right were "fruits" and "vegetables," then "apples" would match with "fruits," and "carrots" would match with "vegetables."

Disk drive	
RAM	Clock
Computer speed	
Accesses memory	Processor
Keyboard	
Data storage	Memory
Execution of program	
Fed instructions	Peripheral
Computer heartbeat	

For additional information on computer hardware, please explore the following websites:

http://www.videojug.com/interview/computer-peripherals-and-
   hardware

http://www.youtube.com/watch?v=HTPQb0EsaXg

Chapter 3:

The evolution of computer language

In the first chapter, we discussed the role of binary, the native language of a computer processor, and how binary language was soon replaced with hexadecimal notation as a less tedious method of programming.

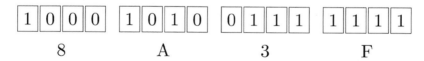

Figure 3.1: Hexadecimal can easily represent large binary numbers.

As you might well imagine, creating a software program—especially a sophisticated program—by entering numeric codes would be a tedious undertaking, and prone to errors and other difficulties. Yet there was a time during the earliest development of computers when entering binary or hex codes by hand was the only option.

It quickly became obvious that an easier method was required, and such a need led to the first development of programming languages.

Assembly

As mentioned in the previous chapter, a computer processor obtains its step-by-step instructions by retrieving numeric codes from sequential locations in memory. For every processor action (math, comparisons, data movement, branching, etc.), there is a specific, numeric code. Natively, these codes are binary, which is not very intuitive (or readable) by humans. This led to the development of the first programming language called *assembly language.*

Assembly language is simply a set of human-readable symbols that represent a processor instruction. For example, a code to compare one byte value to another might be represented in assembly language as "COMP," as in:

```
COMP A, B
```

In this example, "COMP A, B" instructs the processor to compare a value called "A" to a value called "B." The next instruction might be to branch to a new memory location if the comparison results in zero:

```
COMP A, B
BEQ newLocation
```

The two lines above would instruct the processor to compare 'A' to 'B' (COMP A, B) and branch on zero (BEQ) to a memory location called "newLocation," which would be defined elsewhere in the program.

Of course, this "program" is meaningless by itself, and it is serving only as the simplest example of assembly language. The idea is that each processor instruction can be written in "English" symbols instead of the native, numerical codes.

The assembler

A program written in assembly language is really a text file of various symbols and characters, and such text notations are meaningless to a computer processor. Again, the processor requires binary codes to execute instructions. Therefore, a program written in assembly language needs to be translated into numeric instructions that the processor can understand. This translation is possible with an assembler.

An *assembler* is simply a program that will read a text file of assembly symbols, and translate those symbols into machine-readable binary codes. If mistakes were made, the assembler program will abort the translation and report the error(s).

Key point: While assembly has been replaced with more modern languages, the principle remains the same: Your software program, which is a human readable text file, never executes as is, because it must ultimately be translated to machine-readable codes in order to run.

Benefits of textual languages

There are additional benefits to text-based languages versus direct, binary codes. Beside the obvious benefit that text symbols are easier to remember and maintain, a text-based language allows you to easily modify an existing program.

Let's assume that you were one of the earliest programmers who had to enter each processor instruction into memory, byte-by-byte. Let's also assume that various portions of this program referenced specific memory locations (to branch to a new location, for example). What if you needed to insert new instructions in the middle of that program? Such an insertion would invalidate all memory addresses being referenced.

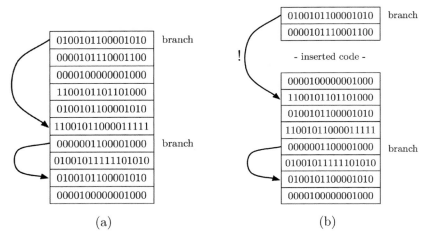

(a)   (b)

Figure 3.2: The difficulty entering computer codes manually. Figure 3.2b illustrates how branch locations would be incorrect after inserting new codes into Figure 3.2a.

Suppose you entered a series of binary codes such as the example in Figure 3.2a. The two locations labeled "branch" are instructions to skip to a specific memory location on special conditions.

The problem is that if you decide to modify this program later on by inserting some new code somewhere in the middle, this will invalidate the branch locations you entered before.

Figure 3.2b shows what can happen if you were to insert a new code inside the old set of codes—the branch locations are no longer valid (the instructions to branch will point to the wrong location since all the codes have been moved). Fixing this program would require finding each "branch" instruction and changing the target location.

Using assembly language (or any higher level language) solves this problem, because memory addresses are also assigned "names."

```
          CMP A,B
          BEQ Location1
          MOV A, #22
          MOV B, #0
Location1
          CMP B,A
          BNE Location2
          CLR A
Location2
```

The example above shows a simple assembly language program that performs two conditional branches. One is to an address that we have named "Location1" and the other called "Location2" (these names were arbitrarily chosen, they can be any unique name). When the assembler converts the program to machine codes, the Location1 and Location2 are resolved to the proper memory locations. Hence, it wouldn't matter if you insert new lines into the program because the assembler would resolve everything for you.

Birth of the compiler

For those who programmed the earliest computers with machine codes, assembly language was a godsend; no longer did a programmer need to enter tedious and error-prone binary statements.

However, it soon became apparent that a better language was needed to create powerful programs. While assembly language made machine programming easier, it was nonetheless *machine* language. Creating large, sophisticated software with assembly was tedious, time consuming, prone to many errors, and difficult to maintain. Worse yet, assembly language was not always portable from one machine to another, because not every computer used the same type of processor.

The need for a more useful language led to the development of the first high-level languages. A *high-level language* is a set of English-like statements that are more intuitive to people than they are to machines. Some of the earlier high-level language included Cobol, a business-oriented language, and Fortran, a mathematical language. Later, a language called Basic was introduced for the earliest desktop computers, then a language called Pascal, and finally, a language called C, which later evolved into C++. Today, C and C++ are the most widely used languages.

Compiler versus assembler

The difference between an assembler and a compiler is that each statement in assembly language corresponds to one (native) processor instruction. Each statement in a higher-level language (such as C and C++) translates to *many* processor instructions. High-level languages need to be translated by a compiler program that breaks each statement down to (sometimes) hundreds of processor codes, and hence, relieves the programmer of the burden to even understand the native machine. High-level languages are also portable—they can be compiled for many different types of processors. C was developed by Dennis Ritchie at Bell Laboratories in 1972, and C++ was developed by Bjarne Stroustrup at Bell Laboratories in 1979.

Below is an example of a simple, high-level language, which is similar to Basic, one of the first languages developed for personal computers.

```
Print "Hello! This is my program."
Print "Please enter your username now."
Input (name$)
If (name = "Joe") goto HelloJoe
Else goto NotKnown

HelloJoe
Print "Hi Joe!"
NotKnown
Print "Hi, we have never met."
End
```

By looking over this small program, you can probably get an idea of what this program is doing, even if you have never seen a program before. But that is the main point—and advantage—of a high-level language: It is generally intuitive and relatively easy to follow.

Of course, this program would never be understood by the computer as is, which is why it would need to be translated by a compiler into the codes that the machine's processor understood.

Exercises

The following statements are excerpts from this chapter. To assure your understanding, write a sentence or two that explains the same thing as the statement but in your own words. Example answers can be found in the appendix.

1. "Your program never executes as is, because it must ultimately be translated to machine-readable codes."

2. "Assembly language is simply a set of human-readable symbols that represents a processor instruction."

3. "The difficulty entering computer codes manually... branch locations would be incorrect after inserting new codes."

4. "A high-level language is a set of English-like statements that is more intuitive to people than to machines."

For additional learning, please explore the following site:

http://en.wikipedia.org/wiki/Programming_language

Chapter 4:

Introduction to C

During the early years of software development, several compiled languages made it to the forefront, each coming and going in popularity. Eventually, "C" became the predominate language, and later, an extension of C called C++. This book will concentrate on C, C++, and later, a hybrid version of C++ called *Objective C* for the Macintosh OS.

Fundamentals

A program in C consists of statements. Each statement does something (arithmetic, comparisons, moving data from one place to another, etc.). With few exceptions, all statements in C must be terminated with a ";" (semicolon):

```
blah blah blah blah;
blah blah blah blah;
```

In fact, if you construct a line without a ";" then the compiler will interpret that line and the next line as one statement:

```
blah blah blah blah
yo ho ho ho;
```

To the human eye, the above two lines might appear to be two separate statements, but the compiler will consider the two lines as a single statement (ignoring the "return" character in between) until it sees the semicolon. The compiler sees:

```
blah blah blah blah  yo ho ho ho;
```

Comments

C allows you to make comments, or "remarks," anywhere in your program, and these comments are ignored by the compiler. A comment is either a single line preceded by a double slash ("//") or a group lines enclosed with "/*" and "*/".

Examples of comments

```
// This program was written to compute my bank balance.
// The compiler will ignore any text preceded by //

/* If I enclose multiple lines inside the asterisk
and slash, the compiler ignores anything inside such
notation */
```

Comments throughout your program are not only important for your own note taking, they are valuable for other programmers who might need to make changes to your files. Always use comments to explain the logic and purpose of major areas of code.

Basic components

The majority of the C language consists of three basic components:

- Variables

- Operators

- Functions

Variables

A variable is a placeholder that contains a value, and it is identified by a name (a name that you invent). A variable name can be any combination of normal alphabetical letters and numbers, upper or lower case, as long as it begins with a letter. Examples of variable names might be "total," "X," "Name," "B2," "myBalance," etc. However, note that variables names are case-sensitive.

In other words, the following two variable names will be considered different names by the compiler:

```
MyBook
Mybook
```

"MyBook" is a different variable than "Mybook" because the second name uses a "b" instead of a "B."

Primitive types

Any variable must be assigned a *data type* in order for it to be valid. Standard data types that most C compilers accept are listed in Table 4.1.

C Type	Description
int	A signed integer (non fractional). The size of the integer varies between some compilers, but typically, an int is a 32-bit, signed value, which implies a range between -2,147,483,648 and +2,147,483,648.
unsigned int	Same as int except the number is unsigned. Hence, a 32-bit int has a range between 0 and 4,294,967,296.
short, unsigned short	Same as int or unsigned int except the value is 16 bits.
long, unsigned long	Same as int or unsigned int except the value is 32 bits.
char	An 8-bit "character." In reality, this can be an 8-bit value from 0 to 255.
double	A double-precision fractional number. Doubles are 64 bits in size.
float	A floating point number.

Table 4.1: The standard data types recognized by C compilers.

In C, variables are declared with the type (one of the above), followed by the variable name, as in the examples in Table 4.2.

C Type	Description
int counter;	An integer called "counter."
double balance;	A fractional value called "balance."
char c;	A character called "c."

Table 4.2: Examples of declaring variables and the meaning of each.

Pointers

A pointer is a memory address of another variable. Quite literally, it "points" to a value somewhere else. A pointer in C is declared with an asterisk ("*") ahead of the variable name:

```
char myChar;     // A single character
char *pMyChar;   // A pointer to a character
```

The difference between the two declared variables is that "my-Char" is a character value, whereas "pMyChar" points to a character somewhere else (the variable names are arbitrary and chosen only for illustration, the "*" notation is what designates one as a pointer). Pointers will be discussed in more detail later in this chapter. For now, it is only important to recognize the different between these types.

Of course, the C "*" notation is valid in front of any variable type:

```
int *pointerToSomeInt;
unsigned int *pointerToUnsigned;
double *pointerToSomeFraction;
```

Arrays

An array is a series of the same variable in a row. You can look at an array as a series of elements, where each element holds its own value.

Arrays are declared in C using brackets:

```
int  myArray[8];      // 8-element wide array
char myString[128];   // 128 characters values
```

A useful aspect of an array is that each element of the array can be indexed, as follows:

```
myArray[0]      //indexes the first element
myArray[1]      //indexes the second element
```

In other words, if myArray is declared as myArray[8], then there are literally 8 elements of int, and each one can be referenced by your program using brackets. What is most useful is that the value inside the brackets can also be another variable:

```
int n;
int myArray[8];
n = 2;
myArray[n] = 0;
```

Operators

Simply stated, an *operator* denotes an operation between variables. Generally, an operator performs either a comparison or an assignment of some value. The simplest example of an operator is the "=" sign:

```
A = 0;
X = A;
```

The "=" sign tells the compiler to assign the value to the right of an equal sign to the variable on the left. In the above example, "A" is assigned the value of 0, and "X" is defined whatever value is contained in "A."

Most of the other operators do a comparison between variables:

```
A > B;   //greater than
A < B;   //less than
A >= B;  //greater than or equal
A <= B;  //less than or equal
A != B;  //not equal
A == B;  //equal
```

Note that the "equal" comparison is designated by two "=" signs, and is not to be confused with the single "=" for an assignment operator. In fact, this is a common error made by beginning C programmers (and even some experienced programmers as well). Consider the following two statements:

```
X = Y;
X == Y;
```

The first statement, "X = Y" causes X to be assigned the same value as Y. The second statement simply compares X and Y together but does not change either of their values. It is important to pay attention to this subtle difference, because to use the wrong one can create program bugs that are difficult to resolve.

There are some additional operators that will be discussed in subsequent chapters. For now, let's see how operators are used within a program.

Conditional statements

A substantial part of a program involves *conditional statements*. A conditional statement is essentially, "If a condition is true, then execute the following statement."

A conditional statement in C always begins with the word "if," followed by the condition to test in parentheses:

```
if (x > 0)
y = 1;
```

The above two lines perform the following. If the variable "x" is greater than zero, then execute the following statement (which is the assignment of "1" to "y").

Carefully note that the first line ("$x > 0$") must not end on a ";" because the compiler treats both lines as part of a single statement. In fact, the following statement performs exactly the same thing as the two lines above:

```
if (x > 0) y = 1;
```

If you did place a ";" character after "if $(x > 0)$," the compiler would interpret the statement entirely differently:

```
if (x > 0);
y = 1;
```

By placing a semicolon after the first statement, the conditional statement does nothing. In effect, you are saying, "if $(x > 0)$, then do nothing," because the ";" character terminates the statement. So, be careful not to make this mistake, because if you do, it could be difficult to understand why your program is behaving erratically.

Blocks

Whenever a statement or series of statements is enclosed in curly braces, the compiler treats all statements inside those braces as a single block of code. A block makes the most sense when used as the executing target of a conditional statement.

Let's say that if a conditional statement is true, you need to execute several more statements. Using curly braces, you can do so as follows.

```
If (y > 0)
{
x - 1;
r = 22;
A = B;
}
```

Unlike our previous example with a single statement following a condition, using curly braces allows you to execute as many statements as needed following the condition. In effect, you are saying, "if $y > 0$, then execute all the statements inside the curly braces."

Braces can also be nested:

```
if (y > 0)
{
x - 1;
r = 22;

if (B > 2)
{
A = B;
}
}
```

The only other aspect to curly braces is that the ending brace does not need to be terminated with a semicolon, because a brace is not a statement, but rather, they enclose statements. The compiler already understands that the "}" character terminates the block.

The "else" statement

Conditional statements can also define an alternative statement (or block of statements) if the condition is false. As we have already learned, if a condition is true (e.g., "if $(y > 0)$"), then the next statement is executed. Using the word "else" will tell the compiler to execute a different statement if the original condition is false. Example:

```
if (x > 0)
y = 1;
else
y = 2;
```

In the above case, if $x > 0$, then assign the value 1 to y; *otherwise* assign the value 2 to y. You can also execute "else" blocks within braces:

```
if (x > 0)
y = 1;
else
{
y = 2;
A = B;
}
```

Functions

A function is a block of code that performs a specific task. Simply stated, a function is a series of statements that will be asked to perform at various times throughout a program.

In fact, all programs begin with an "entry" function, which in turn will invoke more functions. Hence, most of a program consists of functions.

A function is always formatted as follows:

```
[return type] [function name] ([parameters])
{
block of statements within {curly braces}
}
```

The *return type* is an optional value that the function returns when it is executed. If the function doesn't return a value, it should indicate such by stating *void*.

The *function name* is a name (which you invent) that identifies the function. This name can be pretty much anything as long as it doesn't begin with a number. However, the function name must not be the same as another function in the same program file.

The parameters are optional variables that you pass to a function. Parameters must be enclosed in parentheses, and each parameter is separated with a comma (see examples below). If the function doesn't require any variables, you can state void (within parentheses), or with some compilers, you can just state "( )" with nothing inside.

Some function examples:

```
int  getDayOfWeek (int forYear, int forMonth)
{
// This function the day or week based on
//   forYear, forMonth, and forDay.

// The last statement must ''return'' a value:
```

```
return (some integer value);
}

void setMonth (int theMonth)
{
// This function sets the current month
//  to theMonth;

// No return value required.
}
```

Key point: Functions are the very anatomy of a program, and, in fact, functions occupy nearly 100% of most software. While we will discuss functions in more detail in subsequent chapters, it is important to thoroughly understand how to create functions and how they work.

Local versus global variables

Any variable declared within the parameter part of a function is said to be *local* to that function, meaning that only the body of the function (the statements inside the curly braces) can reference them.

Additionally, any variables declared within the body of the function are also local, and can only be accessed by statements inside the curly braces.

A *global* variable is a variable that has been declared outside of the function. Global variables are therefore "global" to all functions. That is, any function can reference them.

The following is an example of local and global variables:

```
int currentYear;

void setMonth (int theMonth)
{
int x;

x = currentYear;
// We can access ''currentYear''
// because it is not defined
// inside another function,
// hence, it is global.

}

int getCurrentYear (void)
{
x = currentYear;

// ERROR! The above will fail to
// compile, because ''x'' is not defined
// within this function,
// nor is it a global variable.

return currentYear;

// Accessing currentYear is OK since
// it is defined globally (outside
```

```
// any function body)
}
```

 # Exercises

The following quiz is designed to consult your understanding of this chapter. The answers are located in the appendix.

1. What is the purpose of a semicolon ";" in a C statement?
2. Describe the difference between a variable and a pointer to a variable. How you designate the difference when declaring either one?
3. What does it mean if you declare the following:

   ```
   int something[16] ;
   ```

4. In a discussion of C statements, if the term "operator" is used, what does that mean? And, give some examples of an operator.
5. What is a conditional operator? Give some examples.
6. What is the meaning of curly braces?
7. Describe the purpose of a function and give a simple example of something a function might do.
8. What is the difference between a global variable and a local variable?

For further understanding of C, please explore the following web sites:

http://computer.howstuffworks.com/c.htm

http://www.cprogramming.com/begin.html

Chapter 5:

Hands-on installation

In order to proceed to the next gradient—actual programming—it will be necessary for you to install a development system on your computer. A development system is a set of software programs that provide the necessary tools to create programs on a specific type of machine. Although there is a lot more programming theory to discuss, it is necessary for you to install the appropriate development system before we can move forward.

If you plan to create programs for Windows, follow the instructions below for "Windows Development." For Macintosh, follow the instructions for "Mac OS-X Development."

After you have successfully installed your development system, proceed to one of the next two chapters: Hands-on for Windows, or Hands-on for Mac OS-X.

Key point: It will be crucial to your training that you partake in every tutorial, followed by theory, to gain the maximum possible understanding.

Windows development

To fully install the Windows development system, follow these steps in the order given.

1. Go to http://www.microsoft.com/express/Downloads/#2008-Visual-CPP on the internet. On this web page, there will be two choices to download, as shown in Figure 5.1. Make sure you choose the download on the left, "Express Edition," not the "Professional Edition."

Figure 5.1: Download page to obtain a Windows development system.

2. The download is a file called "VCSetup.exe." Upon completion of the download, launch VCSetup, which will walk you through the installation. Simply choose all the defaults when it asks for decisions. Note that the installation takes nearly 20 minutes.

3. Proceed to the Chapter 6, "Hands-on for Windows."

Mac OS-X development

To fully install the Mac OS-X development system, follow these steps in the order given.

1. To develop on the Macintosh, your system needs to be at least OS-X 10.6. Apple's development system will not operate on earlier OS versions.

2. You first need to obtain an "Apple ID" as a registered developer before you can download developer tools, which is free of charge. Start by going to the following web address.

   http://developer.apple.com/programs/register.

3. Click the "Get Started" button. The registration is rather long, with survey questions, etc., and you also need to confirm the registration through your email at the end of the process.

4. Once you have registered and have obtained your Apple ID, go to the following web page to download the development system.

   http://developer.apple.com/technologies/xcode.html.

The page you will see should look something like Figure 5.2. There are two choices to download. For now, choose the second one, which I have circled in the image. The page you will be taken to will look like Figure 5.3.

Figure 5.2: Download page for the OS-X development system.

Warning: Pre–release software is Apple confidential information. Your unauthorized distribution of pre–release software or disclosure of information relating to pre–release software (including the posting of screen shots) may subject you to both civil and criminal liability and result in immediate termination of your ADC Membership.

Xcode 3.2.1 Developer Tools Download
Xcode 3.2.1 is an update release of the developer tools for Mac OS X. This release provides bug fixes in gdb, Interface Builder, Instruments, llvm-gcc and Clang optimizer, Shark, and Xcode and must be installed on Mac OS X 10.6 Snow Leopard and higher. Xcode defaults to upgrading an existing Xcode installation but may optionally be installed alongside existing Xcode installations. See accompanying release notes for detailed installation instructions, known issues, security advisories.

Download Name	File Size	Date Posted
About Xcode 3.2.1 (PDF)	68 KB	08 Oct 2009
Xcode 3.2.1 Developer DVD (Disk Image)	751.1 MB	08 Oct 2009

Figure 5.3: Second page of the OS-X download process.

You can download the PDF file if you want (the first entry in Figure 5.3); the development system is the second entry, which is the main download.

5. The download, a DMG (disk image) file, is over 700 megabytes. Once it has been successfully downloaded, double-click the file, which will open into a "disk drive" icon.

6. Open the "drive" icon created by the DMG file. Double-click the file "Xcode.mpkg" to install the development system.

7. Proceed to Chapter 7, "Hands-on for Mac OS-X."

Chapter 6:

Hands-on for Windows

Tutorial 1

If you only intend to develop for the Macintosh and/or the iPhone, you can skip this chapter and proceed to Chapter 7, Hands-on for Mac OS-X.

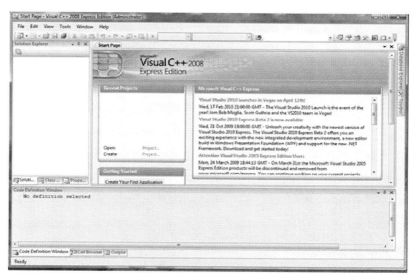

Figure 6.1: Initial screen after launching Visual C++.

After you have successfully installed the Windows development system (instructions in Chapter 5), launch "Microsoft Visual C++

2008 Express Edition," which you can find in your "Programs" submenu in the "Start" menu (bottom-left of your computer). A successful launch should display something similar to Figure 6.1.

For now, we will be creating a very simple program, step by step, followed by a detailed explanation and the purpose of each step.

Step 1: Creating a new project

Starting with the Visual C++ program (as shown above), go to the "File" menu and select "New→Project. . ." as shown in Figure 6.2.

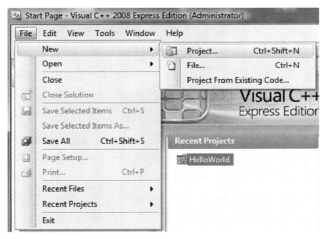

Figure 6.2: Selecting "New Project" in Visual C++.

After you select "New→Project. . ." you are given the choices visible in Figure 6.3.

The left column, "Project Type," will provide three choices. Select "Win32."

The second column will provide two choices in the first row, "Win32 Console Application" and "Win32 Project." Select "Win32

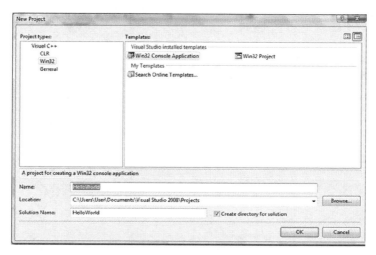

Figure 6.3: Choices for a new project in Visual C++.

Console Application." (This will create a simple program that you will be able to run quickly to see instant results.)

The last step is to give this project a name in the "Name:" field below the two columns. In this case, enter the name, "HelloWorld."

Click OK to complete the project creation. There will be one more window displayed, which confirms your project creation. Click "Finish."

Step 2: Modify the default program

After completing the project creation in Step 1, you will notice that a default project is created.

The left column (titled "Solution Explorer") shows a list of files that will create your program. These are default files that were created for you automatically.

In this tutorial, we will only be concerned with the file, "HelloWorld.cpp" inside the Source Files folder. The contents of this

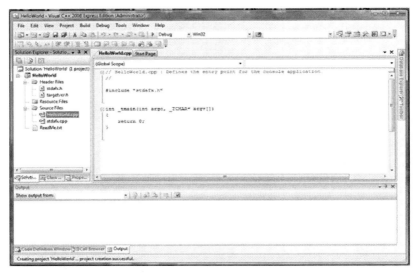

Figure 6.4: The default project created from the *New Project* action

file should be displayed in the larger part of the window, as shown in Figure 6.4. (If not, *double click* on HelloWorld.cpp in the Source Files "folder".)

Click in the text of HelloWorld and add two lines of text after the first "{" so it reads as follows:

```
printf("hello world! My name is <your name>.");
getc(stdin);
return 0;
```

After you have entered this text, it should look similar to Figure 6.5.

Be sure to add the first two lines (substituting <your name> with your first name), leave the 3rd line, "return 0" as is. Be sure that you enter the new text exactly as shown above, but with your own name substituted.

Figure 6.5: The selected file should display the file's contents as shown in this figure.

Step 3: Compile and run the program

Remember, a program is only text until you compile your program file(s). To compile your program, go to the "Build" menu and select "Build Solution."

After your program compiles (builds), you should see some messages in the horizontal box at the bottom of the window. The last line of this message should say the following:

```
======== Build 1 succeeded, 0 failed, 0 up-to-date,
0 skipped
```

If this messages says anything else such as, "====== Build 0 succeeded, 1 failed," that means there was one or more errors.

Figure 6.6: An executable program is created by selecting "Build Solution" from the "Build" menu.

If you have errors:

1. Did you misspell printf or getc? (Note: C is case-sensitive, which means if you used capital letters, such as "Printf," the compiler will not recognize the statement).

2. Did you forget to end a line with a semicolon? (Or did you accidentally type something else, such as a colon?)

3. Did you forget to place quotation marks around the text "Hello World! My name is Joe"?

4. If you find none of the above, carefully compare what you wrote against what is shown above and discover your error.

Once you can do a Build without errors, it is time to run your program.

To run, go to the "Debug" menu and select "Start Debugging". Your program should look like Figure 6.7.

To exit this program, press Return.

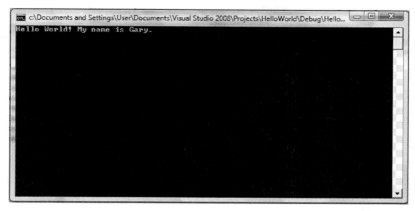

Figure 6.7: Your "Hello World" program should look like this when you run it.

If all went well, congratulations! You have successfully created your first program!

 # Behind the tutorial

The files

When the "HelloWorld" project was started, several files were automatically created for you. The file you modified was named "HelloWorld.cpp" to match the name you gave your project. Had you named your project, "KillerProject," then this file would have been called "KillerProject.cpp."

The file extension ".cpp" is an abbreviation for C++ (C-plus-plus), which we will discuss in more detail later. Some of the other files end in ".h," which denote a *header* file. Header files will also be discussed in subsequent chapters.

Main function

The file you modified contains the default program entry function; in this case it is called _tmain:

```
int _tmain ( int argc, _TCHAR* argv[])
{
}
```

The function, "_tmain," is the *entry point* of your program, which means it is the first function that executes when your program is launched. The function returns an int (integer) value, and it contains two parameters: an int called argc, and an array of character pointers called argv. The purpose of these two parameters is to pass values to your program from a command line, but since our program did not require any parameters from a command line, we ignored both argc and argv.

The code

Let's examine the two lines that you added to the program.

```
printf("Hello World! My name is Gary.");
```

Whenever you create a new project, a standard library of C functions is included automatically. One of the functions in this standard library is *printf*. Basically, printf displays text strings to the console screen. The function, in this case, takes a single parameter, which is a character pointer, or a *string*. When passed as a parameter to a function, a string can be represented with any text between quotation marks. A block of text within quotation marks is also referred to as a *string literal*.

```
getc(stdin);
```

The function *getc* is also part of the standard C library. Essentially, it waits for character(s) to be entered on the keyboard. The one parameter—stdin—is a keyword for "standard input," in this case, the keyboard.

The reason we added "getc" was to force the program to wait. Had we omitted getc, the program would have briefly displayed "Hello World. . ." and then immediately quit. In this tutorial, we didn't care what characters were entered from the keyboard.

Finally, the program ends with one statement.

```
return 0;
```

Simply stated, the function _tmain needs to return an integer value, and, in this case, "return 0" returns the value of zero. Remember, if a function has a variable type ahead of its definition other than "void," it is required to return a value.

For _tmain, the return value informs the system that the program executed successfully, indicated by the value 0. If we returned a non-zero value, the system would assume that the program failed to run properly.

Tutorial 2

For this tutorial, we will be modifying the program again. This time, we will be adding two new files to the project.

To start, launch Visual C++ 2008, and open the HelloWorld project (find it on the "File" menu under "Recent Projects"). Once you have the project open, proceed to the first step below.

Step 1: Add a new source file

A *source file* is a text file that contains program code. In this step, we will add a new source file, also called a ".cpp" file (C++ file).

Click once on the "Source Files" folder (or on a file inside the folder) on the left side of the project window, as in Figure 6.8. Next, go to the "Project" menu and select "Add New Item...," as in Figure 6.9.

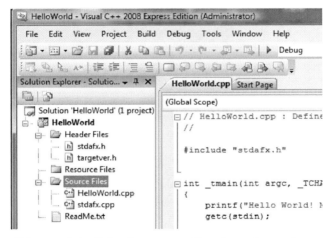

Figure 6.8: Selecting source files from the project.

You should see an "Add New Item" dialog window. First, select "Code" in the left column. Then select "C++ File (.cpp)" in the second column, as shown in Figure 6.10.

Enter the name, "SayHello.cpp" in the Name field near the bottom of the window. Then click "Add."

Step 2: Add a new header file

A header file is a text file that defines items that are referenced by other source files. Header files will be discussed in more detail at the end of this tutorial.

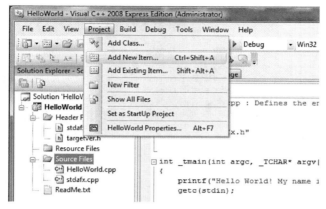

Figure 6.9: Selecting "Add New Item..." will create a new file for your project.

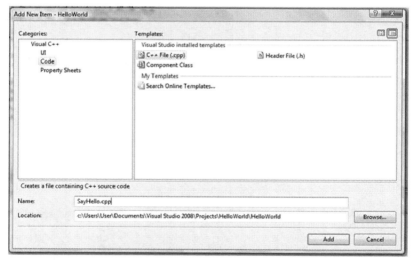

Figure 6.10: Example of selecting a new C++ file to create.

To add a new header file, use the same procedure as in Step 1, except start by clicking in the "Header Files" folder on the project. Then go to the "Project" menu and select "Add New Item..."

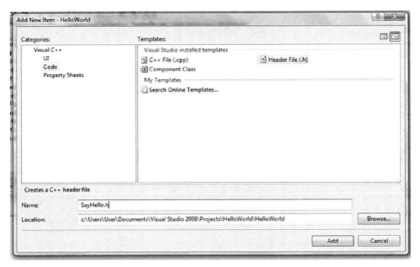

Figure 6.11: Example of choosing a header file (.h) to create.

This time you should select "Header File (.h)" in the right column instead of "C++ File (.cpp)". Name your file "SayHello.h" and click Add.

You should now have two added files: SayHello.cpp (added in Step 1) and SayHello.h (added in Step 2).

Step 3: Modify the added files

Double-click the file, "SayHello.h" in the left column of the project window. This will display a blank file in the larger column on the right. Enter the following:

```
void SayHello (char *message);
```

Next, open "SayHello.cpp" by double-clicking. Enter the following text:

```
#include "stdafx.h"
```

```
#include "SayHello.h"

void SayHello (char *message)
{
printf(message);
}
```

Step 4: Modify the original file (_tmain)

Next, open "HelloWorld.cpp" (double-click). Near the top, enter
the following right below "#include "stdafx.h:"

```
#include "SayHello.h"
```

Finally, remove all the text inside the _tmain function except
for the last line, "return 0" and then enter the following:

```
SayHello("Hello World! My name is Gary.");
getc(stdin);
```

Your HelloWorld.cpp file should now read as follows:

```
#include "stdafx.h"
#include "SayHello.h"

int _tmain(int argc, _TCHAR* argv[])
{
SayHello("Hello World! My name is Gary.");
getc(stdin);

return 0;
}
```

Step 5: Run the program

Go to the "Build" menu and select "Build Solution." The program should build and report no failures. If you get errors, go back and compare all three files to discover what you entered incorrectly. (Pay attention to typical errors, such as missing semicolons or using the wrong case letters.)

After getting the program to build successfully, select "Start Debugging" from the Debug window to run the program. This program will essentially do the same thing as it did in the previous tutorial.

 Behind the tutorial

The tutorial demonstrates the usage of multiple files when constructing a program. Although HelloWorld could easily fit in a single file, most programs that you will create are relatively large, and cramming it all in a single file would make the program difficult to maintain. As a rule, it is easier to create and modify a program if you can break it down to a collection of small files versus one giant file.

Let's examine what occurred in this last tutorial.

Headers

A header file, or a ".h" file, is used to declare functions that are implemented in another file. Using the previous tutorial as an example, we created a function called "SayHello." The function was defined in SayHello.h, but the body of the function was implemented in SayHello.cpp. Notice that the function declaration in the header file terminates with a semicolon, while the function within the .cpp file has statements between curly braces. This is the difference between a function *prototype* and a function *body*.

The purpose of a function prototype is so the compiler will know of its existence without having seen the actual implementation. For example, consider the following program:

```
int shouldWelcome;
if (shouldWelcome == 1)
{
SayHello("Hello to our guest!");
}

void SayHello (char *message)
{
printf(message);
}
```

If you tried to build this program, the compiler would report an error on the third line, "'SayHello' has not been declared." The reason for this error is that the compiler translates your program from the top down, and the function, "SayHello" is defined further down the file from where it is first referenced. Hence, the compiler is not aware of the existence of "HelloWorld" when the first reference to that name is encountered.

One solution would be to move the function to the top of the file.

```
void SayHello (char *message)
{
printf(message);
}
```

```
int shouldWelcome;
if (shouldWelcome == 1)
{
SayHello("Hello to our guest!");
}
```

While the above solution is legitimate C and it would fix the problem, there are times when moving a function to the "correct" place is unrealistic, if not impossible. A better solution—and cleaner C code—is to use the function prototype:

```
void SayHello (char *message);   // prototype

// Other code can go here including
// calls to SayHello()

void SayHello (char *message)  // body
{
printf(message);
}
```

As a rule, your prototype declarations should be placed in header files, which we demonstrated in the previous tutorial with the "SayHello" function.

The tutorial, line by line

First, we created a source file (SayHello.cpp) and a header file (SayHello.h). The purpose of the header file was to declare a function prototype, while the purpose of the .cpp file was to create the body of the function declared in the header.

Within the new file "SayHello.cpp," we added the following two lines at the top:

```
#include "stdafx.h"
#include "SayHello.h"
```

The #include statement is called a compiler directive, which basically tells the compiler to do something special. A compiler directive always begins with a "#" character. In this case, "#include" means to include the specified file during the compilation. Hence, the above two lines tell the compiler to read a file called "stdafx.h" and a file called "SayHello.h" and include those with the program. The file "stdafx.h" was created for you when the project was initially created, and contains special declarations for your program to run properly. We created the other one, "SayHello.h" in the tutorial.

Below the #include statements, we declared a function called "SayHello:"

```
void SayHello (char *message)  // body
{
printf(message);
}
```

Notice that this function performs a similar task to our first tutorial, only this time, it displays whatever character string is passed to the "message" parameter.

Main program

Next, we modified the main program (HelloWorld.cpp). First, we added an #include statement at the top, which is necessary for the compiler to learn of the existence of the function "SayHello."

```
#include "SayHello.h"
```

Next, we altered the code inside _tmain so that our message gets printed to the console by the "SayHello" function:

```
int _tmain(int argc, _TCHAR* argv[ ])
{
SayHello("Hello World! My name is Gary.");
...code...
}
```

You will notice that this version of the program operates identically to the original "HelloWorld" program before alteration, the difference being that the message display occurs within another file, "SayHello.cpp."

Tutorial 3

The purpose of this tutorial is to add a little more complexity to our "HelloWorld" program, and to introduce a few new aspects to C. This time, the finished program will ask for your name and your age, and then it will tell you how old you will be in 15 years.

You will start with the same project as in the previous tutorial, so if you have not done so already, open Visual C++ 2008 and the HelloWorld project.

Step 1: Modify a header

Locate the file, "stdaxf.h" in the Header Files folder, and double click it so that it shows in the editing portion of the window.

Insert "#include <stdlib.h>" so the text reads as follows:

Figure 6.12: Selecting one of the header files in your project.

```
#include "targetver.h"
#include <stdio.h>
#include <stdlib.h>
#include <tchar.h>
```

This change is necessary for the project to build once you are through making all the modifications.

A note on headers

A point that should be mentioned is that an #include file containing quotation marks tells the compiler that the file is located within the project folder or a folder near to the project. A file enclosed in angle brackets tells the compiler that the file resides in the compiler's folder or a system folder. The essential difference between quotation marks and angle brackets is where the compiler looks for the file.

Step 2: Modify the main program

First, you will be adding two function prototypes near the top of the file. Remember, a prototype is a function declaration that will be used later in the file.

Double-click HelloWorld.cpp (so its text appears in the edit portion of the window). Add two function prototypes so the beginning of HelloWorld.cpp looks like this:

```
#include "stdafx.h"
#include "SayHello.h"

void getStringFromKeyboard (char *str);
void printReturn (void);
```

Next, find the function, "_tmain," and replace everything inside the curly braces with the following:

```
char name[128];
char age[128];
int ageIn15;

printf("Welcome!");
printReturn();
printf("Please enter your name: ");
getStringFromKeyboard(name);
printf("Please enter your age: ");
getStringFromKeyboard(age);
printf("In 15 years you will be ");
ageIn15 = atoi(age) + 15;
printf("%i", ageIn15);

printReturn();
printReturn();

getchar();

return 0;
```

Step 3: Add two functions

Somewhere below the _tmain function, add the following two functions:

```
void getStringFromKeyboard (char *str)
{
int i;

for (i = 0; i < 127; i++)
{
int nextChar;

nextChar = getc(stdin);
if (nextChar == '\n')
break;
str[i] = (char)nextChar;
}

str[i] = 0;
}

void printReturn (void)
{
printf("\r\n");
}
```

Full listing

To make sure you have entered all the text correctly, here is a full listing of how HelloWorld.cpp should look:

```
#include "stdafx.h"
```

```c
#include "SayHello.h"

void getStringFromKeyboard (char *str);
void printReturn (void);

int _tmain(int argc, _TCHAR* argv[])
{
char name[128];
char age[128];
int ageIn15;

printf("Welcome!");
printReturn();
printf("Please enter your name: ");
getStringFromKeyboard(name);
printf("Please enter your age: ");
getStringFromKeyboard(age);
printf("In 15 years you will be ");
ageIn15 = atoi(age) + 15;
printf("%i", ageIn15);

printReturn();
printReturn();

getchar();

return 0;
}

void getStringFromKeyboard (char *str)
{
int i;
```

```
for (i = 0; i < 127; i++)
{
int nextChar;

nextChar = getc(stdin);
if (nextChar == '\n')
break;
str[i] = (char)nextChar;
}

str[i] = 0;
}

void printReturn (void)
{
printf("\r\n");
}
```

Step 5: Build and run the program

Select "Build Solution" from the "Build" menu. If you made all the modifications correctly, you should see no failures at the bottom of the screen.

If you have errors:

1. Scroll the bottom portion of the window (the section that reports errors), and find the line(s) that contain the problem(s). For each one, you can double-click the error and it will take you to the offending area.

2. Common errors are mistyping (often not paying attention to upper and lower case), a missing quotation mark, missing parentheses, or a missing semicolon.

3. If you still cannot resolve the errors, start at Step 1 and compare what you have with the tutorial instructions.

If you don't have errors:

Run the program by selecting "Start Debugging..." under the "Debug" menu. The program will ask you for your name; enter your name and then press return key. The program will ask you for your age; enter your age and press the return key. The program should then tell you how old you will be in 15 years.

 ## Behind the tutorial

Let's go over each section of the modified program so you understand the purpose of each addition. The line numbers to the left are provided for your reference. (These numbers do not appear in the actual program.)

```
1 char name[128];
2 char age[128];
```

Lines 1 and 2 are character arrays, or *strings* of 128 elements each. These character arrays will hold the text input from the keyboard. We chose 128 as a nice, round number, but the number could have been any value as long as they were large enough to hold likely keyboard input.

```
3 int ageIn15;
```

Line 3 is an integer that will be used to compute the numeric age + 15 years.

```
4 printf("Welcome!");
5 printReturn();
```

Line 4 simply displays a message to the console. Line 5 calls a function that causes the console to move down one line.

```
6 printf("Please enter your name: ");
7 getStringFromKeyboard(name);
```

Line 6 displays another message as a prompt.

Line 7 calls the function "getStringFromKeyboard," which obtains characters from the keyboard and places them into a character array. In this case, the keyboard input will be placed into the array called "name."

```
8 printf("Please enter your age: ");
9 getStringFromKeyboard(age);
10 printf("In 15 years you will be ");
```

Lines 8 and 9 perform identical tasks to lines 6 and 7, except the keyboard input is placed in "age." Line 10 simply displays a messge.

```
11 ageIn15 = atoi(age) + 15;
```

Line 11 introduces a new function, "atoi" which is defined in a standard C library (similar to how "printf" is also defined in a standard library). The name, "atoi" is an abbreviation for "ASCII-to-integer," which means "translate text to a number."

The reason you need to call "atoi" is because the "age" variable contains text characters, and you need to translate those characters into in integer in order to perform math. In this case, we add 15 to the result of atoi(age).

```
12 printf("%i", ageIn15);
```

Line 12 introduces an additional feature of printf, as follows. Previously, we only passed a single string to printf, as in:

```
printf("Welcome!");
```

However, a "%" character inside the string tells printf that a special format value follows. In the case of:

```
printf("%i", ageIn15);
```

The "i" that follows "%" informs printf that the parameter following the string should be displayed as an integer (in this case, ageIn15). Note that "%i" is not actually displayed, because it is a format instruction. All that displays is the ageIn15 variable. If ageIn15 contained a value of 42, the console would merely display:

```
42
```

This printf feature can also define a format other than integer. The most common ones are:

%i   A signed integer
%u   An unsigned integer
%d   A double
%f   A floating point

```
13 printReturn();
14 printReturn();
15 getchar();
16 return 0;
```

Lines 13 through 16 complete the _tmain function. Lines 13 and 14 add two extra blank lines to the console. Line 15 is added so the console program does not immediately exit, and line 16 returns the function result to the system (0 indicating a successful execution).

Function implementation – printReturn()

```
void printReturn (void)
{
printf("\r\n");
}
```

The printReturn function introduces special characters within a text string. When a string contains a backslash "\" character, the character that follows is a special control character. In this case, \r represents a return character, while \n represents a linefeed character. (In Windows, a full line feed requires a return + linefeed character).

Hence, printReturn() causes the console to print a single, blank line.

Function implementation – getStringFromKeyboard()

```
void getStringFromKeyboard (char *str)
{
int i;
```

```
for (i = 0; i < 127; i++)
{
int nextChar;

nextChar = getc(stdin);
if (nextChar == '\n')
break;
str[i] = (char)nextChar;
}

str[i] = 0;
}
```

Before we discuss each line of this function, there are three new aspects to C that have been introduced.

The for-loop

The getStringFromKeyboard function introduces the *for-loop* for the first time. A for-loop creates a runtime "loop," using the following format:

```
for (<start action>; <condition>; <continue action>)
<statement>;
```

<start action> can be valid statement in C, but usually initializes a variable to some value. The statement within <start action> is executed only once at the start of the loop.

<condition> is a comparison, and if true, the loop continues, otherwise the loop terminates.

<continue action> is a C statement that executes if the loop is to continue.

<statement> is the C statement that executes for each loop. This <statement> can be a single line (terminated with a semi-colon) or can be a series of statements enclosed in curly braces.

Let's look at the for-loop inside getStringFromKeyboard.

```
for (i = 0; i < 127; i++)
```

This for-loop is stating:

1. Execute the statement i = 0 once before the loop begins.
2. Execute the statement that follows as long as i < 127.
3. At the end of each execution, increment i by 1.

In other words, the statement that follows the "for" statement will be executed repeatedly as long as i is less than 127. After each execution, i is incremented by 1.

Inside of a loop, the break statement causes the loop to terminate, regardless of the condition of the loop variables.

```
for (i = 0; i < 127; i++)
{
...code...
break;
}
```

The "++" directive

We have also introduced the "++" directive, which increments a value. Hence, "i++" performs exactly the same thing as:

```
i = i + 1;
```

You can also use "−−" which indicates a decrement, or the equivalent to:

```
i = i - 1;
```

String arrays versus string pointers.

The third aspect that we introduced is the conversion of a string array to a string pointer.

If you look over the entire program, you will notice that each call to getStringFromKeyboard passes a character array, whereas the parameter for the function is defined as a character pointer (char*). Basically, the compiler treats these as identical, and they are often used interchangeably.

The reason is because a char* points to one or more characters, and a character array (as "name[128]") is also a series of characters. Hence, both variables can be indexed in the same way.

```
char array1[128];
char *array2;

Array1[0] = 'a';
Array2[0] = 'a';
```

In both cases, the first element of "array1" and "array2" are assigned the value 'a'. Carefully note, however, that the above code, as is, would cause major runtime problems, because "array2" has not been initialized to anything. To make this work properly, you would need to assign array2 to point to some other buffer of characters before trying to assign values to its content, but this is beyond the scope of the tutorial at this time.

The function, line-by-line

```
1   for (i = 0; i < 127; i++)
```

```
2 {
3 int nextChar;

4 nextChar = getc(stdin);
5 if (nextChar == '\n')
6 break;
7 str[i] = (char)nextChar;
8 }

9 str[i] = 0;
```

Line 1 declares the for-loop, as discussed earlier.

Line 2 begins the statement executed each time the for-loop is "true" ($i < 127$). Because all the code that follows is contained inside curly braces, the for-loop treats the whole block as a single statement. In other words, the entire code block is executed with each pass of the loop as long as the condition of the loop remains true.

Line 3 declares an integer variable that is assigned the value from the keyboard.

Line 4 gets the next character from the keyboard.

Lines 5 and 6 check the character from the keyboard to be equal to a linefeed ("\n"), and if so, the loop terminates with the "break" statement. This is necessary to detect when the return key is pressed.

Line 7 stores the keyboard character into the character array passed to this function. Also introduced is a *cast* directive, "(char)nextChar," which informs the compiler to treat nextChar is a character versus an integer. The purpose of this is that some compilers will issue a warning that you are trying to assign an integer to a character value. Casting the int as a char resolves this warning.

Line 8 terminates the block that is executed by the loop.

Line 9 terminates the string with a zero-value character. This is required for a valid string, also known as a *null-terminated string*.

 # Exercise

Start VisualStudio and create a new project from scratch. You can make the same initial choices that were made in the tutorials. This time, however, see if you can build a new program that displays something else besides "Hello World!"

This exercise is complete when you can start your own project from scratch and have it build and run without errors.

If you wish to explore VisualStudio in more depth, the following website has a wealth of information:

http://www.microsoft.com/express/Resources/

Chapter 7:

Hands-on for Mac OS-X

Tutorial 1

This section should only be used if you intend to develop on an Apple Macintosh. For Windows, start in the section in Chapter 6.

After you have successfully installed the XCode development system (instructions in Chapter 5), locate and launch Xcode. Assuming you installed using all the defaults, Xcode should be on your main drive, as follows:

```
[main drive]Developer/Applications
```

After successfully launching Xcode, you should see something similar to Figure 7.1.

For now, we will be creating a very simple program, step-by-step, followed by a detailed explanation and the purpose of each step. The program will be in the simplest possible form— a command-line program. Later, we will start creating more sophisticated programs.

Figure 7.1: The initial screen after launching Xcode.

Step 1: Creating a new project

Using the opening screen for Xcode (as shown in Figure 7.1), click "Create a new Xcode project" in the left column. A new screen should appear.

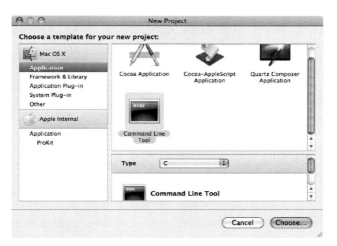

Figure 7.2: Creating a new Xcode project.

In the left column, click Application. In the top-right area, click Command Line Tool. Then click Choose.

After clicking "Choose," the final step is to give your project a name, and a location to save the project. Enter the name "HelloWorld" and save to a location that you will remember.

You have now created a new project.

Step 2: Modify the default program

After completing the project creation in Step 1, you will notice that a default project is created.

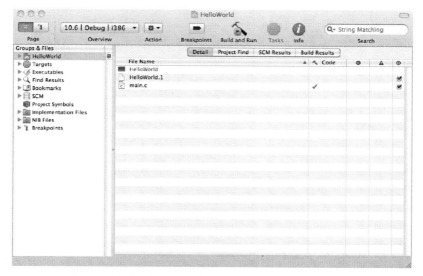

Figure 7.3: A typical project window in Xcode.

The left column, "Groups & Files," shows all the files in the project. All of these files were automatically created for you. Later, you will learn how to add new files.

In this tutorial, we will only be concerned with the file "main.c." To locate this file, click the "arrow" next to HelloWorld, click the arrow next to "Source," and then click on "main.c."

The right half of the window should display the contents of main.c, which will appear as in Figure 7.5.

Figure 7.4: Selecting main.c from the list of files in your project.

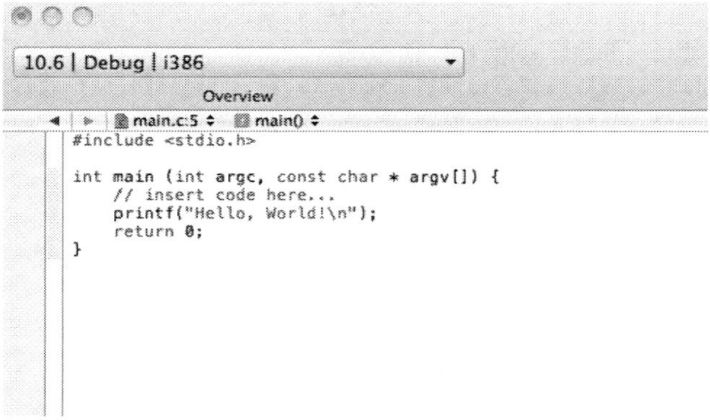

```
10.6 | Debug | i386                          ▼
                    Overview
◀  ▶  ⬛ main.c:5 ⇕  ⬛ main() ⇕
      #include <stdio.h>

      int main (int argc, const char * argv[]) {
          // insert code here...
          printf("Hello, World!\n");
          return 0;
      }
```

Figure 7.5: What your file should look like once modified.

Click in the text and modify the "printf" line to read as below, except substitute <your name> with your name:

```
printf("Hello World! My name is <your name>");
```

Next, add the following line below the "printf" line:

```
getc(stdin);
```

The new text should now look like this:

```
int main (int argc, const char *argv[]) {
// insert code here...
printf("Hello World! My name is <your name>");
```

```
getc(stdin);
return  0;
}
```

Step 3: Build the program

Remember, a program is only text until you compile your program file(s). To compile your program, go to the "Build" menu and select "Build."

If the Build is successful, you will see a message in the bottom-left of the window, "Build successful." If there were errors, the message will say, "Build failed," followed by the number of errors detected. If so, you will need to fix the errors before you can continue.

If you have errors:

1. Did you misspell "printf" or "getc?" (Note: C is case-sensitive, which means if you used capital letters, such as "Printf," the compiler will not recognize the statement).

2. Did you forget to end a line with a semicolon? (Or did you accidentally type something else, such as a colon?)

3. Did you forget to place quotation marks around the text "Hello World! My name is Joe"?

4. If you find none of the above, carefully compare what you wrote against what is shown above and discover your error.

Once you can do a Build without errors, it is time to run your program.

Step 4: Run the program

Since you have created a simple "command line" program, you will need to open a window called "Console" in order to see your program run. To do so, go to the "Run" menu and select "Console." The whole project window will change to two or three divided, horizontal partitions.

Go to the "Run" menu and select "Run."

In the bottom partition, you should see something like Figure 7.6.

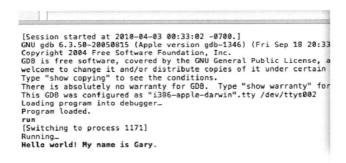

```
[Session started at 2010-04-03 00:33:02 -0700.]
GNU gdb 6.3.50-20050815 (Apple version gdb-1346) (Fri Sep 18 20:33
Copyright 2004 Free Software Foundation, Inc.
GDB is free software, covered by the GNU General Public License, a
welcome to change it and/or distribute copies of it under certain
Type "show copying" to see the conditions.
There is absolutely no warranty for GDB.  Type "show warranty" for
This GDB was configured as "i386-apple-darwin".tty /dev/ttys002
Loading program into debugger...
Program loaded.
run
[Switching to process 1171]
Running...
Hello world! My name is Gary.
```

Figure 7.6: Your program running in the console window.

Notice the last line is displaying the text that you typed into main.c. Although ultra simple, this is your program running!

To exit the program, press Return.

 # Behind the tutorial

The files

The file you modified contains the default program entry function; in this case it is called "main:"

```
int main ( int argc, _TCHAR* argv[])
{
}
```

The function "main" is the *entry point* of your program, which means it is the first function that executes when your program is launched. The function returns an int (integer) value, and it contains two parameters: An int called argc, and an array of character pointers called argv. The purpose of these two parameters is to pass values to your program from a command line, but since our program did not require any parameters from a command line, we ignored both argc and argv.

The code

Let's examine the two lines that you modified or added to program.

```
printf("Hello World! My name is Gary.");
```

Whenever you create a new project, a standard library of C functions is included automatically. One of the functions in this standard library is *printf*. Basically, printf displays text strings to the console screen. The function, in this case, takes a single parameter, which is a character pointer, or a *string*. When passed as a parameter to a function, a string can be represented with any text between quotation marks. A block of text within quotation marks is also referred to as a *string literal*.

```
getc(stdin);
```

The function *getc* is also part of the standard C library. Essentially, it waits for character(s) to be entered on the keyboard. The one parameter—stdin—is a keyword for "standard input," in this case, the keyboard.

The reason we added "getc" was to force the program to wait. Had we omitted getc, the program would have briefly displayed "Hello World..." and then immediately quit. In this tutorial, we didn't care what characters were entered from the keyboard.

Finally, the program ends with one statement.

```
return 0;
```

Simply stated, the function "main" needs to return in integer value, and in this case, "return 0" returns the value of zero. Remember, if a function has a variable type ahead of its definition other than "void," it is required to return a value.

For main, the return value informs the system that the program executed successfully, indicated by the value 0. If we returned a non-zero value, the system would assume that the program failed to run properly.

Tutorial 2

For this tutorial, we will be modifying the program again. This time, we will be adding two new files to the project.

To start, run Xcode and open the HelloWorld project (it should appear on the right side of the start-up window). Once you have the project open, proceed to the first step below.

Step 1: Add a new source file

A *source file* is a text file that contains program code. In this step, we will add a new source file. Therefore, open the Source "folder," click on main.c, then go to the "File" menu and select "New File..."

You will see a dialog window as seen in Figure 7.7.

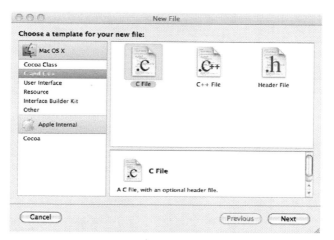

Figure 7.7: Creating a new source file in Xcode.

Click on "C and C++" in the left column, click "C File" in the right column, and then click "Next." The dialog window will appear as in Figure 7.8.

Be sure to provide a name for the new file. In this example, we are using "SayHello.c." Also, make sure the "Also create SayHello.h" is checked.

Click Finish.

Your project will now show two new files added: SayHello.h and SayHello.c.

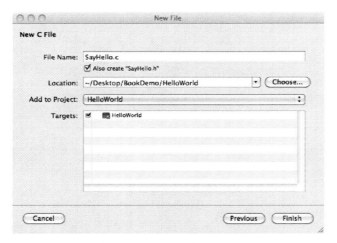

Figure 7.8: Specifying the C file name to create.

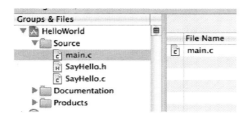

Figure 7.9: Choosing "main.c" means you want to view or modify this file.

Step 2: Modify the added files

Click the file "SayHello.h." Add the following lines to this file:

```
#include <stdio.h>
```

```
void SayHello (char *message);
```

Save changes to this file with File→Save (or command-S).

Next, click "SayHello.c." After the statement, "#include "Say-Hello.h,"enter the following text:

```
void SayHello (char *message)
```

```
{
printf(message);
}
```

Save your changes to SayHello.c.

Step 3: Modify the original program file (main)

Next, open "main.c." Near the top, right below "#include <stdio.h>," enter the following:

```
#include "SayHello.h"
```

Finally, change "printf" with SayHello, so it reads like this:

```
SayHello("hello world! My name is <your name>.");
getc(stdin);
```

Your main.c file should now read as follows.

```
#include <stdio.h>
#include "SayHello.h"

int main(int argc, _TCHAR* argv[])
{
SayHello("hello world! My name is Gary.");
getc(stdin);

return 0;
}
```

Step 4: Run the program

Go to the "Build" menu and select "Build." The program should build and report no failures. If you get errors, go back and compare all three files to discover what you entered incorrectly. (Pay attention to typical errors such as missing semicolons or using the wrong case letters.)

After getting the program to build successfully, open the Console from the "Run" menu, then select "Run" from the Run window to run the program.

This program will essentially do the same thing as it did in the previous tutorial.

 ## Behind the tutorial

The tutorial demonstrates the usage of multiple files when constructing a program. Although HelloWorld could easily fit in a single file, most programs that you will create are relatively large, and cramming it all in a single file would make the program difficult to maintain. As a rule, it is easier to create and modify a program if you can break it down to a collection of small files versus one giant file.

Let's examine what occurred in this tutorial.

Headers

A header file, or a ".h" file is used to declare functions that are implemented in another file. Using the previous tutorial as an example, we created a function called "SayHello." The function was defined in SayHello.h, but the body of the function was implemented in SayHello.c. Notice that the function declaration in the header file terminates with a semicolon, while the function within the .cpp file has statements between curly braces. This is the difference between a function *prototype* and a function *body*.

The purpose of a function prototype is so the compiler will know of its existence without having seen the actual implementation. For example, consider the following program:

```
int shouldWelcome;
if (shouldWelcome == 1)
{
SayHello("Hello to our guest!");
}

void SayHello (char *message)
{
printf(message);
}
```

If you tried to build this program, the compiler would report an error on the third line, "'SayHello' has not been declared." The reason for this error is that the compiler translates your program from the top down, and the function, "SayHello" is defined further down the file from where it is first referenced. Hence, the compiler is not aware of the existence of "HelloWorld" when the first reference to that name is encountered.

One solution would be to move the function to the top of the file:

```
void SayHello (char *message)
{
```

```
printf(message);
}

int shouldWelcome;
if (shouldWelcome == 1)
{
SayHello("Hello to our guest!");
}
```

While the above solution is legitimate C and it would fix the problem, there are times when moving a function to the "correct" place is unrealistic, if not impossible. A better solution—and cleaner C code—is to use the function prototype:

```
void SayHello (char *message);    // prototype

// Other code can go here including
// calls to SayHello()

void SayHello (char *message)   // body
{
printf(message);
}
```

As a rule, your prototype declarations should be placed in header files, which we demonstrated in the previous tutorial with the "SayHello" function.

The tutorial, line by line

First, we created a source file (SayHello.c) and a header file (SayHello.h). The purpose of the header file was to declare a function prototype, while the purpose of the .c file was to create the body of the function declared in the header.

Within the new file, "SayHello.h" we added the following line at the top:

```
#include <stdio.h>
```

The #include statement is called a compiler directive, which basically tells the compiler to do something special. A compiler directive always begins with a "#" character. In this case, "#include" means to include the specified file during the compilation. Hence, the above line tells the compiler to read a file called "stdio.h" before it compiles the program. (The file "stdio.h" defines some standard system functions that the program will use.)

Below the #include statement, we declared a function called "SayHello:"

```
void SayHello (char *message)
{
printf(message);
}
```

Notice that this function performs a similar task to our first tutorial, only this time, it displays whatever character string is passed to the "message" parameter.

Main program

Next, we modified the main program (main.c). First, we added an #include statement at the top, which is necessary for the compiler to learn of the existence of the function, "SayHello."

```
#include "SayHello.h"
```

Next, we altered the code inside "main" so that our message gets printed to the console by the "SayHello" function.

```
int main(int argc, _TCHAR* argv[])
{
SayHello("hello world! My name is Gary.");
...
}
```

You will notice that this version of the program operates identically to the original "HelloWorld" program before alteration, the difference being that the message display occurs within another file, "SayHello.c."

Tutorial 3

The purpose of this tutorial is to add a little more complexity to our "HelloWorld" program and to introduce a few new aspects to C. This time the finished program will ask for your name and your age, and then it will tell you how old you will be in 15 years.

You will start with the same project as in the previous tutorial, so if you have not done so already, open Xcode and the HelloWorld project.

Step 1: Add a header

Open the file main.c and insert "#include <stdlib.h>" right after "#include <stdio.h>" so the text reads as follows:

```
#include <stdio.h>
#include <stdlib.h>
#include "SayHello.h"
```

This change is necessary for the project to build once you are through making all the modifications.

A note on headers

A point that should be mentioned is that an #include file containing quotation marks tells the compiler that the file is located within the project folder or a folder near to the project. A file enclosed in angle brackets tells the compiler that the file resides in the compiler's folder or a system folder. The essential difference between quotation marks and angle brackets is where the compiler looks for the file.

Step 2: Modify the main program

First, you will be adding two function prototypes near the top of the file. Remember, a prototype is a function declaration that will be used later in the file.

Open "main.c" and add the following two lines after the #include statements:

```
void getStringFromKeyboard (char *str);
void printReturn (void);
```

Next, find the function, "main," and replace everything inside the curly braces to the following:

```
char name[128];
```

```
char age[128];
int ageIn15;

printf("Welcome!");
printReturn();
printf("Please enter your name: ");
getStringFromKeyboard(name);
printf("Please enter your age: ");
getStringFromKeyboard(age);
printf("In 15 years you will be ");
ageIn15 = atoi(age) + 15;
printf("%i", ageIn15);

printReturn();
printReturn();

getchar();

return 0;
```

Step 3: Add two functions

Somewhere below the main function, add the following two functions:

```
void getStringFromKeyboard (char *str)
{
int i;

for (i = 0; i < 127; i++)
{
```

```
int nextChar;

nextChar = getc(stdin);
if (nextChar == '\n')
break;
str[i] = (char)nextChar;
}

str[i] = 0;
}

void printReturn (void)
{
printf("\r\n");
}
```

Full listing

To make sure you have entered all the text correctly, here is a full listing of how main.c should look:

```
#include <stdio.h>
#include <stdlib.h>
#include "SayHello.h"

void getStringFromKeyboard (char *str);
void printReturn (void);

int main (int argc, const char * argv[]) {
char name[128];
char age[128];
int ageIn15;
```

```
printf("Welcome!");
printReturn();
printf("Please enter your name: ");
getStringFromKeyboard(name);
printf("Please enter your age: ");
getStringFromKeyboard(age);
printf("In 15 years you will be ");
ageIn15 = atoi(age) + 15;
printf("%i", ageIn15);

printReturn();
printReturn();

getchar();
return 0;
}

void getStringFromKeyboard (char *str)
{
int i;

for (i = 0; i < 127; i++)
{
int nextChar;

nextChar = getc(stdin);
if (nextChar == '\n')
break;
str[i] = (char)nextChar;
}

str[i] = 0;
```

```
}

void printReturn (void)
{
printf("\r\n");
}
```

Step 4: Build and run the program

Select "Build Solution" from the "Build" menu. If you made all the modifications correctly, you should see no failures at the bottom of the screen.

If you have errors:

- Scroll the bottom portion of the window (the section that reports errors), and find the line(s) that contain the problem(s). For each one, you can double-click the error, and it will take you to the offending area.
- Common errors are mistyping (often not paying attention to upper and lower case), a missing quotation mark, missing parentheses, or a missing semicolon.
- If you still cannot resolve the errors, start at Step 1 and compare what you have with the tutorial instructions.

If you don't have errors:

Run the program by first selecting "Console" from the "Run" menu, and then selecting "Run" under the "Run" menu. The program will ask you for your name; enter your name and then press return key. The program will ask you for your age; enter your age and

press the return key. The program should then tell you how old
you will be in 15 years.

Behind the tutorial

Let's go over each section of the modified program so you understand the purpose of each addition. The line numbers to the left
are provided for your reference (these numbers do not appear in
the actual program). .

```
1 char name[128];
2 char age[128];
```

Lines 1 and 2 are character arrays, or *strings* of 128 elements
each. These character arrays will hold the text input from the
keyboard. We chose 128 as a nice, round number, but the number
could have been any value as long as they were large enough to
hold likely keyboard input.

```
3 int ageIn15;
```

Line 3 is an integer that will be used to compute the numeric
age + 15 years.

```
4 printf("Welcome!");
5 printReturn();
```

Line 4 simply displays a message to the console. Line 5 calls a
function that causes the console to move down one line.

```
6 printf("Please enter your name: ");
7 getStringFromKeyboard(name);
```

Line 6 displays another message as a prompt.

Line 7 calls the function "getStringFromKeyboard," which obtains characters from the keyboard and places them into a character array. In this case, the keyboard input will be placed into the array called "name."

```
8 printf("Please enter your age: ");
9 getStringFromKeyboard(age);
10 printf("In 15 years you will be ");
```

Lines 8 and 9 perform identical tasks to lines 6 and 7, except the keyboard input is placed in "age." Line 10 simply displays a message.

```
11 ageIn15 = atoi(age) + 15;
```

Line 11 introduces a new function "atoi" which is defined in a standard C library (similar to how "printf" is also defined in a standard library). The name "atoi" is an abbreviation for "ASCII-to-integer," which means "translate text to a number."

The reason you need to call "atoi" is because the "age" variable contains text characters, and you need to translate those characters into in integer in order to perform math. In this case, we add 15 to the result of atoi(age).

```
12 printf("%i", ageIn15);
```

Line 12 introduces an additional feature of printf, as follows. Previously, we only passed a single string to printf, as in:

```
printf("Welcome!");
```

However, a "%" character inside the string tells printf that a special format value follows. In the case of:

```
printf("%i", ageIn15);
```

The "i" that follows "%" informs printf that the parameter following the string should be displayed as an integer (in this case, ageIn15). Note that "%i" is not actually displayed, because it is a format instruction. All that displays is the ageIn15 variable. If ageIn15 contained a value of 42, the console would merely display:

```
42
```

This printf feature can also define a format other than integer. The most common ones are:

%i   A signed integer
%u   An unsigned integer
%d   A double
%f   A floating point

```
13 printReturn();
14 printReturn();
15 getchar();
16 return 0;
```

Lines 13 through 16 complete the main function. Lines 13 and 14 add two extra blank lines to the console. Line 15 is added so the console program does not immediately exit, and line 16 returns the function result to the system (0 indicating a successful execution).

Function Implementation – printReturn()

```
void printReturn (void)
{
printf("\r\n");
}
```

The printReturn function introduces special characters within a text string. When a string contains a backslash "\" character, the character that follows is a special control character. In this case, "\r" represents a return character, while "\n" represents a linefeed character. (A full line feed requires a return + linefeed character).

Hence, printReturn() causes the console to print a single, blank line.

Function implementation – getStringFromKeyboard()

```
void getStringFromKeyboard (char *str)
{
int i;

for (i = 0; i < 127; i++)
{
int nextChar;

nextChar = getc(stdin);
if (nextChar == '\n')
break;
str[i] = (char)nextChar;
}
str[i] = 0;
}
```

Before we discuss each line of this function, there are three new aspects to C that have been introduced.

The for-loop

The getStringFromKeyboard function introduces the *for-loop* for the first time. A for-loop creates a runtime "loop," using the following format:

```
for (<start action>; <condition>; <continue action>)
<statement>;
```

<start action> can be any valid statement in C, but usually initializes a variable to some value. The statement within <start action> is executed only once at the start of the loop.

<condition> is a comparison, and if true, the loop continues; otherwise the loop terminates.

<continue action> is a C statement that executes if the loop is to continue.

<statement> is the C statement that executes each time the loop is executed. This <statement> can be a single line (terminated with a semicolon) or can be a series of statements enclosed in curly braces.

Let's look at the for-loop inside getStringFromKeyboard.

```
for (i = 0; i < 127; i++)
```

This for-loop is stating:

1. Execute the statement i = 0 once before the loop begins.
2. Execute the statement that follows as long as i < 127.
3. At the end of each execution, increment i by 1.

In other words, the statement that follows the "for" statement will be executed repeatedly as long as i is less than 127. After each execution, i is incremented by 1.

Inside of a loop, the *break* statement causes the loop to terminate, regardless of the condition of the loop variables.

```
for (i = 0; i < 127; i++)
{
...code...
break;
}
```

The "++" Directive

We have also introduced the "++" directive, which increments a value. Hence, "i++" performs exactly the same thing as:

```
i = i + 1;
```

You can also use "−−" which indicates a decrement, or the equivalent to:

```
i = i - 1;
```

String arrays versus string pointers.

The third aspect that we introduced is the conversion of a string array to a string pointer.

If you look over the entire program, you will notice that each call to getStringFromKeyboard passes a character array, whereas the parameter for the function is defined as a character pointer (char*). Basically, the compiler treats these as identical, and they are often used interchangeably.

The reason is because a char* points to one or more characters, and a character array (as "name[128]") is also a series of characters. Hence, both variables can be indexed in the same way.

```
char array1[128];
char *array2;

Array1[0] = 'a';
Array2[0] = 'a';
```

In both cases, the first element of "array1" and "array2" are assigned the value 'a'. Carefully note, however, that the above code, as is, would cause major runtime problems, because "array2" has not been initialized to anything. To make this work properly, you would need to assign array2 to point to some other buffer of characters before trying to assign values to its content, but this is beyond the scope of the tutorial at this time.

The function, line-by-line

```
1   for (i = 0; i < 127; i++)
2 {
3 int nextChar;

4 nextChar = getc(stdin);
5 if (nextChar == '\n')
6 break;
7 str[i] = (char)nextChar;
8 }

9 str[i] = 0;
```

Line 1 declares the for-loop, discussed earlier.

Line 2 begins the statement executed each time the for-loop is "true" ($i < 127$). Because all the code that follows is contained inside curly braces, the for-loop treats the whole block as a single statement. In other words, the entire code block is executed with each pass of the loop as long as the condition of the loop remains true.

Line 3 declares an integer variable that is assigned the value from the keyboard.

Line 4 gets the next character from the keyboard.

Lines 5 and 6 check the character from the keyboard to be equal to a linefeed ("\n"), and, if so, the loop terminates with the "break" statement. This is necessary to detect when the return key is pressed.

Line 7 stores the keyboard character into the character array passed to this function. Also introduced is a *cast directive*, "(char)nextChar," which informs the compiler to treat nextChar as a character rather than an integer. The purpose of this is that some compilers will issue a warning that you are trying to assign an integer to a character value. Casting the int as a char resolves this warning.

Line 8 terminates the block that is executed by the loop.

Line 9 terminates the string with a zero-value character. This is required for a valid string, also known as a *null-terminated string.*

Exercises

1. One of the best ways to learn how to develop software is to use pre-built examples. When you installed your Xcode system, there should have been a folder created on your main disk drive in a "Developer" folder. Open Developer and look for an Examples folder. Within that folder, there should be some Xcode example projects (they will end with ".xcodeproj"). Double-click any one of these of interest, build, and run.

2. Make some modification somewhere, even if minor, and see if you can still build the program with your changes!

For more information on Xcode, please visit the following Apple site:

http://developer.apple.com/tools/xcode/xcodeprojects.html

Chapter 8:

More C

This chapter applies to both Windows and Mac OS development, and it covers several more aspects to C. Some of this information has been briefly mentioned in previous chapters, while some of the information is new.

Loops

A program *loop* is a series of statements that get executed repetitively as long as a specific condition is true. There are various forms of a loop in C, but they all have a process, and a condition upon which to repeat.

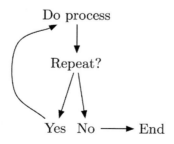

Figure 8.1: The logic of a "loop" in C.

The for-loop

The for-loop will repeatedly execute any block of code as long as a condition (that you specify) remains true. The loop always begins with the word "for," followed by three optional statements inside parentheses, and then followed by the code that should execute for each loop.

The following is a simple example:

```
int   x;
for (x = 0; x < 100; x++)
{
    ...code...
}
```

In the above example, the first statement within the parenthesis $(x = 0)$ sets the variable x to zero. The second statement $(x < 100)$ is the condition for which the loop should continue. In other words, as long as x is less than 100, the loop will continue to execute. The third statement (x++) increments x by one each time the code block is executed. The code block is whatever exists inside the curly braces.

The sequence of execution is as follows:

1. x is set to zero ("$x = 0$").

2. if x is less than 100, the code block between the curly braces is executed.

3. x is incremented by one (x++) after the code block executes.

4. Steps 2 and 3 are repeated.

Once the condition in Step 2 is false, the loop terminates.

Using the for-loop

A common use of the for-loop is to "walk through" an array, although the for-loop can be used for anything.

Suppose your program defined an array of 500 characters, and you wanted to set each character to zero. This could be done efficiently using a for-loop:

```
char myArray[500];
int i;

for (i = 0; i < 500; i++)
{
myArray[i] = 0;
}
```

The for-loop above continues to execute the code block (in this case, it is a single statement, "myArray[i] = 0"). The variable i is incremented for each pass. Once i reaches 500, the loop is terminated.

The while-loop

The while-loop is similar to the for-loop except it tests a single condition. As long as the condition remains true, the code block that follows will execute repeatedly.

```
char myArray[500];
int i;
i = 0;
while (i < 500)
{
myArray[i] = 0;
```

```
i++;
}
```

In the above example, the code block continues to execute as long as the stated condition remains true (in this case, i being less than 500). Note an important distinction, however. Unlike the for-loop, you would need to initialize the variable i to its starting value prior to the loop. Otherwise, its value would be uninitialized and uncertain. Also, you would need to increment i within the code block. Otherwise, the loop would never terminate (because i would remain less than 500 forever).

The do-while loop

Sometimes you might want to test the loop condition at the end of your code block instead of its beginning. In this case, you can use the do-while loop.

```
char myArray[500];
int i;
i = 0;
do
{
myArray[i] = 0;
i++;
} while (i < 500);
```

The above example is almost identical to the regular while-loop except for one minor difference: The code block is executed at least once, regardless of the condition, because the condition to continue the loop is tested at the end of the code block instead of the beginning.

The break

Sometimes you might want to terminate a loop regardless of condition. You can do so using the *break* statement. Consider the following example:

```
int findOneCharacter (char *inString, char theChar)
{
int index;

for (index = 0; index < 256; index++)
{
if (inString[index] == theChar)
break;
}

return index;
}
```

The function findOneCharacter returns the position in inString for the character theChar. In this example, inString is known to be 256 bytes in length, and hence, your loop would need to traverse through a maximum of 256 characters. If a match is found, however, you would want to terminate the loop. The break statement does just that—it breaks out of the loop unconditionally.

The break statement can be used within any type of loop.

Infinite loops

There is an occasion when you might want a loop that continues forever unless an exact condition occurs. One example might be to continue monitoring the keyboard until a certain key is typed.

Infinite loops can be created in several ways. Using the for-loop, you can simply create empty statements in the loop declaration.

```
for (;;)
{
...code...
}
```

In the above loop, since there is no condition statement, the loop would continue forever. Of course, somewhere in your code you would need to provide a break statement to terminate the loop. Otherwise, the loop would execute eternally.

A simpler way to create an infinite loop is to declare a while-loop with a condition that is always true.

```
while (1)
{
...code...
}
```

The above while-loop continues forever, because the value "1" is always true (non-zero). Again, your code would need to provide a break statement somewhere to escape the loop. Otherwise, the code would repeat for eternity.

The switch

There is another statement in C called the *switch* statement. Consider the following code that checks for various values of a variable called *total*.

```
If (total == 0)
{
...code...
}
else
if (total == 10)
{
...code...
}
else
if (total == 16)
{
...code...
}
else
{
...code...
}
```

The code above, while technically correct, can become cumbersome, particularly when you have a very long list of possible values to test. C provides a more convenient method for testing many conditions of a value through the *switch* statement.

```
switch (total)
{
case 0:
...code...
break;

case 10:
...code...
```

```
break;

case 16:
...code...
break;

default:
...code...;
break;
}
```

The above example performs exactly the same thing as the previous "if-then" example, except it is cleaner and easier to maintain. The switch statement tests the value of the variable provided (in this case, *total*), and executes the *case* statement that matches. Notice the term *default* as one of the "cases." This is the case that will execute if none of the other case values match. The default statement is optional, and if omitted, the entire switch statement will do nothing if no cases match.

Note that each case statement contains the word *break*. The purpose of the break statement is that the code would continue to execute beyond its case if *break* were omitted. Most of the time, you would not want execution to continue beyond its case statement, but there are situations when you might want execution to continue.

Considering the following example:

```
switch (total)
{
case 0:
...code...
```

```
case 10:
...code...

case 16:
...code...
break;

default:
...code...;
break;
}
```

The switch statement above is identical to the first example, except that the break statement has been omitted from case 0 and case 10. In this case, if the value of *total* were 0, then the code for case 0 *and* case 10 *and* case 16 would execute, because the processor is not told to "break" out of the switch statement. If the value of *total* were 10, the code under case 16 would also execute. So you need to be very careful with this (unless it is intended), otherwise your program might contain bugs that are difficult to find.

Defining types

In addition to the standard variable types in C, you can also define your own types by using the *typedef* command:

```
typedef <type>  <new type>;
```

where <type> is a variable type already defined, and <new type> is a name that becomes an equivalent type of <type>.

For example, the following statement declares a new type called "myType," and it is of type "int":

```
typedef int myType;
```

This tells the compiler that "myType" is the same as an "int," which means you can start using myType instead of int if you so choose:

```
int someValue;
myType anotherValue;
```

The above two statements are both integers, because myType has been defined as an int.

Why would you ever need to define your own types? Typically, you would do this for clarity. Consider the following definition that declares a pointer to a character string:

```
char *somePointer;
```

If this were your only pointer in a program, additional clarity would probably be unnecessary. However, suppose your program had many different pointer declarations, in which case, you might lose track of what each pointer refers to. In this case, you might consider doing something like this:

```
typedef char* namePtr;
```

The above statement declares that the type namePtr is the same as a character pointer (char *). You can probably ascertain that a "namePtr" most likely is used to point to a string that contains a "name." Hence, using namePtr throughout your program would clarify what type of pointer it is. This can provide clarity, especially in very large programs.

The mighty macro

A commonly used directive in C is the *macro*. A macro declares a term that will get automatically substituted with another statement. The simplest version of a macro is a one-item substitution.

```
#define myValue 22
```

The keyword #define tells the compiler that a macro is being declared. The term that follows is the macro's name, and the third term is the statement to be substituted wherever "myValue" is used. Carefully note that there is no ";" (semicolon) for a macro statement, because this is a directive to the compiler and not a statement of code.

Consider the following statement:

```
#define myValue 22

int x;
x = myValue;
```

When the compiler sees "myValue," it knows that the "22" should be substituted. Hence, in this case, the variable x is being assigned the value of 22.

One common use for the macro is to define constant values that can be used repeatedly throughout the program but with the option to change that value to something else at a later date.

For example, suppose you have defined a matrix of numbers of 10 rows and 10 columns wide. You might want to define the size of each column and row using macros.

```
#define numRows     10
#define numColumns 10
```

Using macros for your row and column sizes is a good ideabecause you might want to change one of these dimensions later. For example, if you referenced the row size 30 different times in your program, without defining a macro, you would need to find every place you referenced this number and change every one of them.

Using a macro, however, would require you to change only the value in the macro itself (in this case, "numRows"). Instantly, all occurrences of "numRows" would magically change.

Macro variables

In addition to simple substitution, you can also add variables to the definition. Consider the following.

```
#define addOne(v)    v=v+1
```

Note that the "(v)" that immediately follows the macro, "addOne." This tells the compiler to substitute "v" in the statement with whatever variable is provided in your code. For example:

```
int counter;

addOne(counter);
```

The statement, "addOne(counter)" causes the compiler to invoke the macro definition and substitute "v" with the variable "counter." In other words, the above statement is identical to this:

```
int counter;

counter = counter + 1;
```

Key point: Macros should be used sparingly, or at least they should be kept simple. Excessive use of complicated macros makes debugging or maintaining your program very difficult and often more trouble than it's worth.

Structures

A *structure* in C is a group of variables that define a record. Consider the following definition that represents some bank account information:

```
typedef struct {
int accountNumber;
double prevBalance;
double debit;
double credit;
double endBalance;
}bankRecord;
```

The above statements represent a structure called "bankRecord." Any structure you define should look similar to this, except the members of the structure (in this case, "accountNumber," "prevBalance," etc.) might be different. Following this definition, you would access this structure called "bankRecord" as follows:

```
bankRecord theAccount;
theAccount.accountyNumber = 3724112;
theAccount.prevBalance = 10000;
theAccount.debit = 0;
theAccount.credit = 125.25;
theAccount.endBalance = prevBalance - theAccount.debit
    + theAccount.credit;
```

Why use structures?

The advantage of structures is that you can pass groups of variables as a single parameter, using a pointer. Consider the following code:

```
void initAccount (bankRecord  *theAccount, int accountNum)
{
theAccount->accountNumber = accountNum;
theAccount->prevBalance = 0;
theAccount->debit = 0;
theAccount->credit = 0;
theAccount->endBalance = 0;
}


bankRecord theAccount;
initAccount(&theAccount, 101607);
```

In the above example, we created a function, "initAccount," which accepts a pointer to an accountRecord structure. This functions sets the account number and initializes all the other values to zero. Below this function, a call is made for this initialization, passing an accountRecord as &theAccount.

 # Exercises

The following questions have been designed to consult your understanding of this chapter. The answers are in the Appendix.

1. What is wrong with the following loop?
   ```
   for (;;)
   {
   x = x + 1;
   }
   ```
2. Write a simple "while" loop that repeats exactly 8 times, using a single int value called "x."

3. When is it beneficial to use a "switch" statement instead of a series of "if-then-else" statements?

4. State a reason why you might want to define your own variable type. For example, think of a reason you might want to define a new type of "int."

5. Name at least one reason why you would want to use a macro to define a numeric value. Example: #define offsetToName 22.

6. Name at least one advantage of using a struct (structure) instead of discrete, individual variables.

7. Show an example of defining a "struct" with one int, one double, and one character array of two[2] characters.

For more in-depth information on C structure, macros, and loops, explore the following web sites:

http://www.cprogramming.com/tutorial/cpreprocessor.html

http://www.dreamincode.net/forums/topic/13919-understanding-loops-in-c/

Chapter 9:

Introduction to C++

So far, we have explored the various features of C, but an extension of C, called C++, is increasingly used as the language of choice.

Variables, structures, and functions

The simplest way to explain C++ is to first cover the purpose of three major components of C: Variables, structures, and functions. Consider the following C code that we covered in the previous chapter:

```
typedef struct {
int accountNumber;
double prevBalance;
double debit;
double credit;
double endBalance;
}bankRecord;

void initAccount (bankRecord *theAccount,
    int accountNum)
{
theAccount->accountNumber = accountNum;
```

```
theAccount->prevBalance = 0;
theAccount->debit = 0;
theAccount->credit = 0;
theAccount->endBalance = 0;
}

bankRecord anAccount;

int main ()
{
initAccount(&anAccount, 1000);
}
```

The function main() makes a call to initAccount(), passing anAccount as an argument. The function initAccount() initializes the bankRecord to an account number and some zeros. While this is legitimate C, there are several disadvantages to this code, namely:

1. The variable "anAccount" is global in scope, meaning that it is accessible by every other function in this program. While that might seem like an advantage, it can become problematic if the program becomes large and complex. For example, if you decided to maintain several hundred "account records," program bugs could accidentally write into the wrong record.

2. It would be difficult to dynamically allocate more than one account record. Using the methods shown above, you would need to either declare a lot of individual account records, or you would need to think of some scheme to allocate each one dynamically in memory (such as an array of bankRecord).

3. Assuming you would need to create many more functions to manipulate a bankRecord, you would need to pass this record to every function that worked on the data.

Each of these limitations can be overcome with C++.

The class

The heart of C++ is called a *class*. Stated as simply as possible, a class is a structure with functions, and the composite of these elements act as a single group. This "group" can then be referenced throughout your program as a single entity—instead of referring to each element or each function separately.

The following is an example of a class declaration that will perform the same task as our earlier C example:

```
class bankAccount
{
public:

bankAccount (accountNum);
~bankAccount ();

int accountNumber;
double prevBalance;
double debit;
double credit;
double endBalance;
};
```

Let's go over the above declaration line by line.

class bankAccount: This tells the compiler that the following code within the curly braces is a C++ class.

public: : This is a C++ class keyword that informs the compiler the data within the class is accessible by other parts of the program. If we omitted this keyword, the data within the class would be accessible only to the class itself.

bankAccount (accountNum): This is a special function called a constructor (see below).

~bankAccount (): This is a special function called a destructor (see below).

accountNumber through **endBalance**: Variables that this class "holds" in the same way as in our previous struct examples.

Constructors and destructors

A C++ class definition is simply a definition or a "template." This definition, by itself, creates no data or code implementation. Later, when a class is declared as a variable, it is said to be *instantiated*, meaning that the class becomes a live data structure that can be accessed by your program.

Upon instantiation, the *constructor function* is called automatically.

A simple example of "instantiating" a class would be to declare a variable of the class type:

```
bankAccount myAccount;
```

The mere presence of "myAccount," of type "bankAccount" creates an instance of "bankAccount."

The constructor of any class is always the same name of the class itself. In this case, the constructor function is called bankAccount, and it takes one parameter—an "account number." Of course, your class can declare a constructor with any number of parameters, or none at all.

The destructor function of a class is also declared with the same name of the class, except it has a "~" in front of it. The destructor is called when the instantiation goes out of scope (more on this concept later).

Generally, you use the constructor function to initialize your class, and the destructor function to clean anything up before the class disappears (releasing allocated memory, for instance).

Key point: C++ is not really a different language. Rather, it is an extension and enhancement to C. The easiest way to understand C++ is to envision a list of functions and variables that are all encapsulated into a single, named group called a class. Using C++ can help you organize your C programs, save you from a lot of extra work, and help you minimize programming bugs.

Becoming an instance

There are two ways a class is instantiated in your program. The first way is to simply use it as a variable.

```
bankAccount myAccount(1001);
```

The above line instantiates the bankAccount class, and, by doing so, the constructor is called automatically (the function "bankAccount()"). Note that this declaration itself is also a call to the constructor, so you will need to pass the required parameters. In the above example, we pass the "account number" that the bankAccount class expects.

Once the class is instantiated, it can be referenced as a structure:

```
int accountNum;
double balance;

accountNum = myAccount.accountNumber;
balance = myAccount.endBalance;
//... etc.
```

The second (and a more common way) to instantiate a class is to use a keyword "new." The word "new" is recognized by the compiler, and it creates an instance of your class that is allocated to memory:

```
bankAccount *myAccount;

myAccount  = new bankAccount(1001);
```

Note that the difference between using "new" versus declaring the class as a variable is that "new" will return a pointer to the instance of your class, which is why we declared it as *myAccount. You would therefore access its data using pointer operations:

```
accountNum = myAccount->accountNumber;
balance = myAccount->endBalance;
//... etc.
```

Also note that your constructor function is called when you instantiate it with "new."

When you no longer want a class instance created with "new" to be around anymore, you can remove it from memory using "delete:"

```
delete  myAccount;
```

This will cause the allocated instance "myAccount" to be removed from memory. Prior to its removal, its destructor function will be called.

CAUTION: Once you delete a class that was previously created with "new," it is no longer valid; any attempt to access it will cause your program to fail.

Scope

A class that has been instantiated is said to be in scope. This means that its data is accessible by parts of your program outside of the class. An instance is said to go out of scope when one of two things occur:

1. When declared as a variable, the instance goes out of scope when the program exits the block of code within curly braces. Example:

```
void showAccount (void)
{
```

```
bankAccount theAccount(1001);

printf(bankAccount.accountNumber);
}
```

Since theAccount is declared inside the above function, it goes out of scope once the function has completed and returns to the caller. As it goes out of scope, its destructor function is called.

2. When created with "new," the instance is deleted:

```
theAccount = new bankAccount(1001);
//...more code.
delete theAccount;
```

The delete operator will cause the instance to go out of scope, at which time, its destructor function is called.

Implementation

So far, we have shown two function declarations in the class definition—the constructor and destructor, but each function requires an implantation (code that executes when these get called). Implementing functions declared in a C++ class are created as follows.

```
bankAccount::bankAccount (int accountNum)
{
theAccount->accountNumber = accountNum;
theAccount->prevBalance = 0;
theAccount->debit = 0;
theAccount->credit = 0;
theAccount->endBalance = 0;
}
```

```
bankAccount::~bankAccount ()
{
}
```

The two functions above implement the constructor and destructor for bankAccount, respectively, and these can exist anywhere in your program as long as the compiler is aware of the class definition. Notice that each function is prefaced with "bankAccount::" which informs the C++ compiler that the implementation belongs to the class "bankAccount." In this example, the constructor is initializing values within the class, while the destructor does nothing.

Organization

Generally, your class definitions should be contained in header files (.h files), while your implementation code for each class should be contained in separate source files (.cpp for "C++"). Using the #include directive, the two are hooked together:

```
#include "bankAccount.h"
```

In the case of our bankAccount class, the class definition is stored in "bankAccount.h," while the implementation for the class is in "bankAccount.cpp."

Key point: Technically, you can name your source files anything you want, but make sure your C++ implementation files end with a .cpp extension. Most compilers require this extension to "know" that the code inside the file is C++ and not C.

Additional functions

You can declare additional functions inside a class as long as you remember to implement them. In the following example, we will add the function, "setAccountNumber()."

```
class bankAccount
{
public:

bankAccount (accounNum);
~bankAccount ();

void setAccountNumber (int accountNum);

int accountNumber;
double prevBalance;
double debit;
double credit;
double endBalance;
};
```

The implementation might look something like this:

```
void bankAccount::setAccountNumber (int accountNum)
{
accountNumber = accountNum;
}
```

Notice that this implementation also requires "bankAccount::" in front of the function so that the compiler knows to what class the code belongs. One difference between this implementation and the constructor/destructor functions is the word "void." Constructors and destructors do not require a function result, but all other class functions do. Hence, we had to declare "void" (or whatever the function result might be) in front of setAccountNumber().

What might also be noted is that the variable "accountNumber" is known to the compiler as a variable exclusive to the class, "bankAccount." This is one of many advantages to C++, because the class variables are always available to any function for that class. In C, you would need to declare "accountNumber" either globally, or as one of the function parameters.

Multiple instances

One of the most powerful features of C++ is the fact that you can make multiple instances of the same class, but you only need to implement the class functions once. Using the "bankAccount" class as an example, consider the following:

```
bankAccount *account1;
bankAccount *account2;
bankAccount *account3;

account1 = new bankAccount(0);
```

```
account2 = new bankAccount(0);
account3 = new bankAccount(0);

account1->setAccountNumber(1022);
account2->setAccountNumber(1035);
account3->setAccountNumber(1051);
```

Since each instance of bankAccount holds its own copy of the "account number," each of them can be set to different numbers, even though there is only one function implementation – "setAccountNumber()." If we looked into the memory of account1, account2, and account3, we would see the accountNumber variables set to 1022, 1035, and 1051, respectively.

Overloading

Another powerful feature of C++ is called overloading.

Overloading means that you can declare two or more functions of the same name, but each with different parameters. Consider the following two functions that might be declared in "bankAccount."

```
class bankAccount
{
...
void setAccountNumber (int accountNum);
void setAccountNumber (char *accountNum);
}
```

Note that each function has the name "setAccountNumber." This would normally be illegal in C because you cannot declare two functions of the same name. In C++, this is allowed, and the compiler decides which function to call based on the values you pass to the parameters. If you made a call like this:

```
myAccount->setAccountNumber(1022);
```

The compiler would conclude that you are calling the function that accepts an int as its argument, because "1022" is clearly a numeric value. If you made this call:

```
myAccount->setAccountNumber("2211");
```

The compiler would call the second function named "setAccountNumber" because the second function accepts a character string. Note that if you use overloading, you must implement each function separately. Then you let the compiler decide which function will be called at runtime.

Parents and children

A powerful feature in C++ is the ability for one class to include all the definitions of a previous, or "parent" class. In C++, this is called *inheritance*.

Let's use our bankAccount class to illustrate inheritance.

```
class ATMTransaction  :  bankAccount
{
ATMTransaction (int accountNum);
};
```

The above declaration of "ATMTransaction" looks like any other class definition, except it tells the compiler that "bankAccount" is its parent class. This means that all definitions contained in "bankAccount" are automatically included in the definition for "ATMTransaction."

In other words, the "ATMTransaction" class is a variation of "bankAccount." It is still a basic "bankAccount" class, but with added details for "ATMTransaction."

ATMTransaction is said to be a subclass of bankAccount.

For example, if you created an instance of "ATMTransaction," the following would be legal:

```
ATMTransaction *myATM;

MyATM = new ATMTransaction (0);
MyATM->setAccountNumber(1022);
```

Note that the class definition of ATMTransaction does not define the function "setAccountNumber," but its parent class (bankAccount) does. Hence, the function is also available to any instance of ATMTransaction.

Inheritance in C++ is used mostly to refine a class to something more specific. An example would be a class called "Food," with subclasses of different food types. The "Food" class would contain common data for all food, while the individual subclasses might be "Meat," "Vegetables," and "Grains."

Function overriding

Whenever you create a subclass, all definitions of the parent class are automatically inherited into the new definition. As stated in the examples above, if we created a subclass of "bankAccount," the function "setAccountNumber" (defined in bankAccount) is automatically accessible to instances of the subclass.

There are situations, however, when you will want the subclass to implement the same function a little differently. This can be accomplished by the keyword *virtual*.

```
class bankAccount
{
virtual void setAccountNumber (int accountNum);
};
```

Note the keyword "virtual" in front of bankAccount's definition of the function, "setAccountNumber." This tells the compiler that any subclass of bankAccount can have its own declaration of setAccountNumber. Of course, you will need to declare the same function in "ATMTransaction" for this to occur.

```
class ATMTransaction : bankAccount
{
void setAccountNumber (int accountNum);
};
```

In your implementation of the main class and the subclass, you would provide code for both functions.

```
void bankAccount::setAccountNumber (int accountNum)
{
}

void ATMTransaction::setAccountNumber (int accountNum)
{
}
```

At runtime, the appropriate function is called, depending on the class of the instance being referenced. If the instance is type "bankAccount," then the first function above is called. If the type is "ATMTransaction," the second function is called.

In this way, you can control what happens for each subclass—an extremely powerful feature.

More C++

We covered some of the basic features of C++ that are necessary for understanding subsequent chapters. More advanced features exist in the language, and you are encouraged to study additional materials that provide a more comprehensive approach to this language. For more information on these topics, please see Chapter 13.

 Exercises

The following quiz is designed to assess your understanding of this chapter. The answers are located in the appendix.

1. What is the basic difference been a "struct" in C versus a class in C++?

2. What does it mean to instantiate a class?

3. Name at least one way to instantiate a class.

4. What is a constructor function, and when is it called?

5. What does it mean when a C++ instance "goes out of scope?"

6. Since it is legal to have identical names for two or more functions in a C++ class, how does the compiler know which one to call when it is referenced?

7. What does "inheritance" mean in C++?

For more in-depth C++ material, explore the following site:

http://www.cplusplus.com/doc/tutorial

Chapter 10:

Real world applications

A few years ago, a chapter on "real world" applications would be covering how to create desktop applications for your PC or Mac. However, technology has evolved to a point where your desktop computer and the internet have become nearly interchangeable.

In fact, the increasing popularity of smart mobile devices (iPhone, Android, and recently, the iPad) is evidence of this evolving technology. For this reason, we will devote the final chapters to programming a mobile device.

For purposes of demonstration, we will choose development for the Apple iPhone, since the state of iPhone development at the time of this writing offers the fastest, easiest path to a running application. Additionally, learning iPhone programming immediately opens the door to applications for its close cousin—the iPad.

In fact, the only real difference between programming for an iPhone versus an iPad is the available "real estate" for your screen. Since both devices use the same operating system, targeting either device is a simple setting in your development project.

Getting started with iPhone

The first thing you need to do is to obtain an Apple Macintosh computer to create your software. The minimum requirements will be an Intel-based processor and at least OS-X 10.6.2. If you already have the hardware requirements, you can upgrade your OS to 10.6.2 or above.

In order to program for the iPhone and/or iPad, you will need to become a registered developer via the iPhone/iPad Software Development Kit (SDK). First we will show you how to register for free, to get access to technical resources, tools, and information for developing with iOS, Mac OS X, and Safari. Then we will go through the steps for registering for $99 or more.

Key point: You cannot install your program on an iOS device until you are a registered developer in the Apple iOS Developer Program. This is the $99 option explained in this chapter. The "free" option is only recommended if you simply want to experiment creating iPhone and iPad applications. Once you decide to create genuine applications to run on these devices, you will need to register with the paid option.

The free option

Go to http://developer.apple.com/programs/register/ and click on
the "Get Started" button (Figure 10.1). Choose "Create an Apple
ID," and then click Continue (Figure 10.2).

Figure 10.1: Apple developer registration page.

Figure 10.2: Step one for signing up as an Apple developer.

You will need to create an Apple ID and password and fill out
the required information. When you have this completed, click on

the "Continue" button located on the bottom right of the page. Remember to save your Apple ID and password to be used later.

Figure 10.3: Completing your "personal profile" when registering as a developer.

Figure 10.4: Confirmation of Apple developer registration.

Upon completion, you will be sent an email to confirm your account. Follow the instructions on the email, which will complete the registration process.

You are now registered as an Apple developer.

The $99 or More Option

The $99 option allows you to install your applications onto real devices. Additionally, you will have access to the Apple stores, plus additional support and more resources. If you are only learning, or do not plan to distribute your apps for real devices, the "free" option might be suitable.

Go to http://developer.apple.com/programs/ios/ and click on the "Enroll Now" button.

Figure 10.5: First screen for the $99 developer option.

Follow the instructions provided on this website. They will be nearly identical to the "free" option, but with a little more information. Like the free option, this process is completed once you respond to the email sent to you for confirmation.

Download the development software

Use your newly created Apple ID to log in to the iOS Dev Center at http://developer.apple.com/devcenter/ios/index.action. Under the Downloads section, select "Xcode 3.2.4 and iOS SDK 4.1."

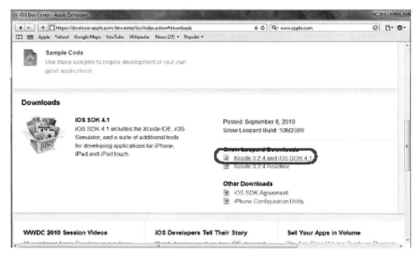

Figure 10.6: The download page for Apple development software.

Once you have downloaded Xcode and iOS SDK, make sure you run the package installer (which will be inside your download) and that the software has installed successfully.

You are now ready to develop iPhone and iPad applications!

Chapter 11:

Basic iPhone programming

Both the iPhone and iPad devices operate on a system called iOS, which is a modified version of Macintosh OS-X. And, like Mac OS-X, programs are developed with a language called Objective-C.

While a thorough course in Objective-C is beyond the scope of this book, we will cover enough basics to get you started. Note that additional materials exists on Apple websites, and we will make references to this material throughout this—and subsequent chapters.

Objective-C basics

Objective-C is an offshoot of the C language, but with C++-like features. The term *objective* is derived from the word "object," since the essence of Objective-C is the creation and manipulation of object modules.

An object

In Chapter 9, we discussed the concept of creating a "class" in C++. Objective-C is similar, but it uses a different syntax. In this respect, an "object" and "class" are synonymous. The proper syntax to define an object is as follows:

```
@interface Name : Inherited
{
}
<function definitions>

@end
```

An object definition always starts with "@interface" and ends with "@end," with other definitions in between.

For the @interface declaration, "Name" is the name of your object, and "Inherited" is the object from which this new object is derived from. In Objective-C for Macintosh and iOS, the most basic object is called "NSObject."

Hence, if the name of your object were "MyObject," the object definition would look like this:

```
@interface MyObject : NSObject
{
}
```

You will declare variables that are available to the object inside the curly braces. This is similar to declaring variables inside a C++ class. For example, if you wanted to make a couple of integer variables as part of your object, it might look like this.

```
@interface MyObject : NSObject
{
int mValue1;
int mValue2;
}
```

In the above declaration, the variables "mValue1" and "mValue2" are accessible to the implementation code of the object, but not to any code outside of the object.

Objective-C Methods

In C++, you can embed functions (also called methods) inside a class. Similarly, in Objective-C, you can create functions that belong to the object, only in this case, they are called "messages."

"Messages" (functions) are declared outside the curly braces, but before the "@end" statement, and require the following syntax:

```
- (return value) functionName;
```

The "return value" is an optional return value, in parentheses following a "-" (dash). If there is no return value, it should read, "- (void)." If the function has no arguments, the definition is terminated with a semicolon.

If the function has one or more arguments, the above statement should list the arguments as follows:

```
:(type)argumentName   argumentName:(type)argumentName;
```

The first argument follows the function name with a ":" and a (type), such as an integer or a string followed by the name of the argument. If there are additional arguments, they are declared as argumentName:(type) argumentName. Technically, the two argument names can be different. (The one on the left is referenced by the calling code, while the one on the right is referenced by the object implementation.) For clarity, it is a good practice to use the same name.

If you are declaring, say, two arguments of type char* in the function, "myFunction," it would look like this:

```
-(void) myFunction:(char*)arg1   arg2:(char*)arg2;
```

Whole Definition

Using all the above examples, the entirety of an object declaration would look something like the following:

```
@interface MyObject : NSObject
{
int mValue1;
int mValue2;
}

-(void) myFunction:(char*)arg1   arg2:(char*)arg2;

@end
```

The implementation

Object declarations (as in the previous example) are generally within header (.h) files. In Objective-C, the implementation is generally contained in a file with a ".m" extension. The implementation content for the example given for "MyObject" should look like this:

```
#import "MyObject.h"

@implementation MyObject
```

```
-(void) myFunction:(char*)arg1  arg2:(char*)arg2
{
}

@end
```

On the top of the file, '#import "MyObject.h"' tells the compiler to include the header file "MyObject.h." Note that "#import" and "#include" do the same thing, except "#import" is a unique compiler directive for Objective-C.

The implementation of all declared functions are created between "@implementation MyObject" and "@end." In this case, we have one function—myFunction—which would contain code between the curly braces.

Making the call

Functions are called in Objective-C with a slightly different syntax than C++. Calls to any object must use the following syntax:

```
[object function:value1 argument2:value2
    argument3:value3];
```

where "object" is the Objective-C object, and "function" is the name of the function defined for the class. If the function has arguments, the first argument follows a ":" and the remaining arguments are given as "name:value" pairs, where "name" is the name of the argument, and "value" is the value of the argument.

Creating an object

In order to call a function within an object, the object has to be created in the first place. In C++, you create a class with the "new" directive. In Objective-C, you create objects using "alloc":

```
MyObject *obj;

obj = [[MyObject alloc]init];
```

The function name, "init" is the default function for allocation, and it is declared in NSObject (the common denominator class for all Objective-C objects). However, your object can define a different initialization function, and you can call that instead when you perform an "alloc."

Note that the resulting object from this call is a pointer to the object, and hence, its implementation is created in memory. Once you are done using the create object, you destroy it with the "release" function.

```
[obj release];
```

Treasure trove

Objective-C for the Mac OS (which includes the iPhone and iPad) is called Cocoa. Within Cocoa is a large treasure chest of built-in objects. Many objects begin with the prefix, "NS" (as in NSObject), which is an abbreviation for NextStep (the original Object-C for Macintosh). When dealing with iOS, many of the standard objects begin with "UI" (an abbreviation for User Interface).

NSObject	This is the most primitive object of all, and in fact, almost all objects in Cocoa and iOS are derived from NSObject.
NSString	Most programs will use NSString extensively, and it will serve you well to learn all about it. An NSString provides a wealth of functions to create and manipulate character strings.
UIView	Nearly all user interface items inside an iPhone or iPad are some version of UIView. Such things as images, buttons, and even a window are offspring of the UIView object. It will be important to learn as much about this object as possible. (Note: In the Mac OS, this object is called NSView.)
NSArray	This object holds an "array" of any NSObject. In many programs, you will find many uses for an NSArray.
NSData	An NSData object holds general data as a buffer of bytes. This is useful for general file reading and data manipulation.

Table 11.1: Common Objective-C objects.

It is beyond the scope of this book to cover all of the standard objects provided in Cocoa. However, we cover a few of the most commonly used objects here and show how to look up reference material for others.

Reference Material

The best way to find reference materials for any Cocoa object is to locate the object name with Google. For example, I entered "NSString" for a Google search, and the first item was "NSString Class Reference," which is exactly what I wanted. Usually, you will find the Class Reference document within the first five or six found items in this search.

A full primer

The Apple development center has an excellent primer on Objective-C at the following web address:

http://developer.apple.com/library/ios/navigation/index.html

On the above page, click the link, "Learning Object-C: A primer." This material is highly recommended to obtain a comprehensive grasp of the language.

Exercise

An excellent series of documents are available on the Apple development site that will explain the concepts for iPhone development in good detail. To begin this study, load the same page as given above (http://developer.apple.com/library/ios/navigation/) and then click the link, "Creating an iPhone Application."

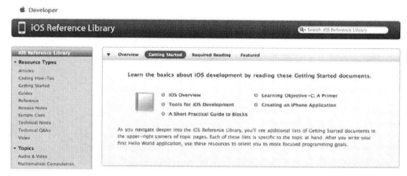

Figure 11.1: The iOS center for learning material.

Understanding the material in "Creating an iPhone Application" is crucial for successful iPhone programming. Once you feel your understanding is sufficient, proceed to the next chapter.

Chapter 12:

A roadmap to applications

The fastest way to become a seasoned pro at iPhone/iPad development is to begin with applications that already exist. Fortunately, there are many examples readily available for this purpose, with detailed documentation, and you can begin by visiting the following web page:

http://developer/apple.com/library/ios/#samplecode/MoveMe/
   Introduction/Intro.html

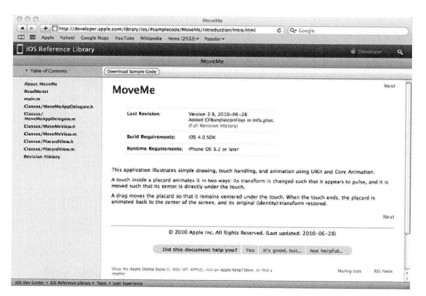

Figure 12.1: A sample iOS program reference, downloadable for full access.

Click the "Download Sample Code" button in the upper left. Assuming you have already installed the Xcode development system, double-click the file, "MoveMe.xcodeproj" which will launch Xcode and open this sample project.

Once the MoveMe project is open, press Command-R (which is "Build and Run"). The program will build, and it will launch into the iPhone simulator. Play with this application for a few minutes to get an idea what it does. Then, quit the program and return to the web page in Figure 12.1.

This time, click "Next," which is on the right side of the page. Walk through the documents and look over the information, as this is an excellent tutorial on how this program and programming the iPhone in general work.

Key point: Developing for the iPad versus the iPhone is essentially identical. The only difference is the device target setting in your project. When running on the iPad, you have more "real estate" for your screen area than the iPhone. Otherwise, both devices use the same operating system.

Targeting iPad

To change the target device to an iPad, open the Project Info window. (Double-click on the top line in the left column of your project.) Find the line for "Targeted Device Family." Clicking in the second column will present a "popup" menu from which you can select iPad. Re-build your project, and it will instantly be targeted for the new device.

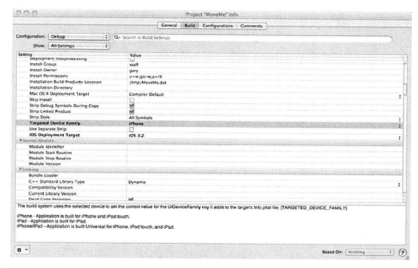

Figure 12.2: The settings window. Use this window to change the targeted device.

More samples

More often than not, it is easier to modify an existing program to obtain your desired results versus starting one from scratch. For this reason, it is highly recommend that you examine the examples provided in Table 12.1 and choose the one that most closely resembles an application you would like to create.

To obtain samples, go to the following link:

http://developer.apple.com/library/ios/navigation

On the left side, find and click the link, "Sample Code," and it will take you to a long list of sample programs. Each program has a detailed description for each component as well as a "Download Sample Code" button.

Usually, you will find an example that is close enough to an application you want to develop, and the working example is an excellent template to start. Some of the more interesting samples are given below.

HelloWorld	Demonstrates how to use a keyboard to enter text into a text field and how to display the text in a label. This is a good starting point and is a bit more sophisticated than our own "HelloWorld" in previous chapters.
ZoomingPDFViewer	Shows how to build a PDF file viewer.
PhotoScroller	Demonstrates how to display photos that can be individually panned and zoomed.
Breadcrumb	Demonstrates how to use iPhone features to track a user's location.
MixerHost	Demonstrates processing audio and sound in an iPhone application.
GLPaint	Demonstrates how to support single finger painting and some motion detection.
Avouch	Demonstrates how to play an audio file.
WeatherMap	Demonstrates how to display maps. It demonstrates creating fictitious weather information for some major cities.
QuickContacts	Demonstrates creating an address book using various modules in the iPhone development system.
MoviePlayer	Demonstrates how to play full-screen movies.

Table 12.1: A list of sample applications that can be downloaded.

Installing on devices

Key point: You cannot install your program on an iOS device until you are a registered developer in the Apple iOS Developer Program. This is the $99 option explained in Chapter 10.

The iPhone development system provides an iPhone simulator for testing. When you are ready to try your application on a real iPhone, take the following steps.

1. Launch the Xcode project for the product you wish to install onto an iPhone or iPad device.

2. By default, your Xcode project is set to run in the iPhone simulator. To change this, double-click the top line in the left column (the project name). This will present the "Project Info" window.

3. Select the second column in the "Base SDK" row. It should present the options in Figure 12.4.

   Change the setting from "iOS Simulator" to one of the devices under "iOS Device SDKs." This tells the Xcode compiler to build your program to run on the actual device instead of the simulator.

   Close the "Project Info" window.

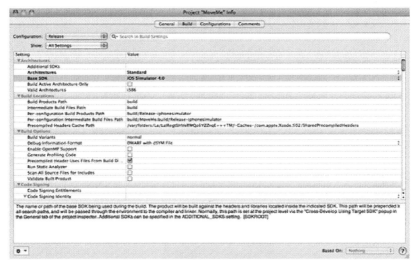

Figure 12.3: The project Info window.

Figure 12.4: The "popup" menu to select which device to target your application

4. From the "Window" menu, select "Organizer." You should see a screen that looks similar to Figure 12.5. Make sure the "Automatic Device Provisioning" is selected at the top.

5. Plug in the device (iPhone, iPad, etc.) to your computer that you wish to target. Once the computer recognizes the

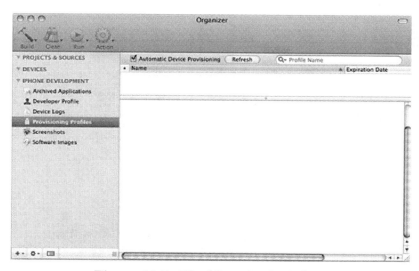

Figure 12.5: The "Organizer" window.

device, it should appear under the "Devices" section as in
Figure 12.6. Note that Figure 12.6 is showing an iPod, but
this could be an iPhone or iPad as well.

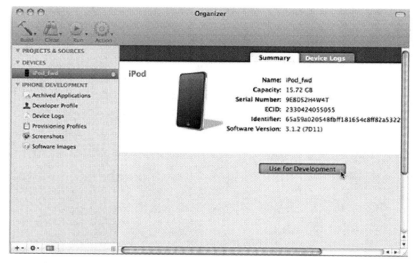

Figure 12.6: A typical view of the "Organizer" window when a device is
recognized.

6. Click "Use for Development." The dialog that comes up
   will want your credentials for iOS Developer Program. Once
   those are entered, Xcode adds the new device to your project.
   Xcode also adds a profile called, "Team Provisioning Profile"
   to your device. This provisioning profile is shared among the
   members of your team (if other people besides yourself work
   on these projects).

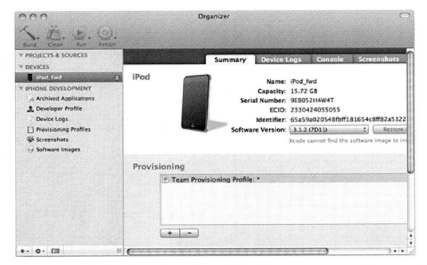

Figure 12.7: The final window when configuring your program for a specific
device.

If Xcode offers to request a development certificate in your
behalf, click Submit Request.

To ensure that your device is provisioned correctly, you can
download a sample project, build it using a device SDK, and run
the application it produces on your device.

Exercise

Choose any one of the sample programs listed in this chapter. Launch the sample project in Xcode, build, and run. Then quit the program and find a place you can modify it in order to see a visual difference in the program (it could be a word, or position of a box, etc.). Continue this exercise until you can build one of the samples with your modification, without error, and that your changes can be seen somewhere in the running program.

See Chapter 13 for an extensive list of resources for additional learning.

Chapter 13:

Where to go from here

The intent of this book is to provide enough underlying information for you to continue your education independently. There is a vast reservoir of information available on the worldwide web, and the following guide is provided to assist you in getting started.

C and C++ learning sites

The following is an excellent site for beginners, including an "Ask the Experts" link. If you can get beyond the ad clutter, this is a good resource for answering basic questions:

http://www.cprogramming.com

You might also consider some of the literature in the following bibliography:

C++ for Dummies, Stephen R. Davis, John Wiley & Sons
Thinking in C++, Bruce Eckel, Prentice Hall
Effective C++, Scott Meyers, Addison-Wesley
The C++ Standard Library, Nicolai M. Josuttis, Addison-Wesley

Objective-C learning

If you are developing for the Macintosh or mobile devices (iPhone, iPad), the following is a decent site for Objective-C, including tutorials:

http://cocoadevcentral.com/d/learn_objectivec

The following is the official website for iOS (iPhone/iPad) development; it includes a link to an excellent primer on Objective-C:

http://developer.apple.com/library/ios/navigation

Developing for Android

The following is the "official" site to develop for the Android mobile device; it contains vast material to get started and to produce apps for this instrument:

http://developer.android.com/guide/index.html

The following site helps tie Android development with Google ad-ons:

http://code.google.com/android

Microsoft Windows Development

The following is a Microsoft website for beginning developers; it contains many resources and documents for beginners, complete with videos and several entry levels:

http://msdn.microsoft.com/en-us/beginner/default.aspx

The following is Microsoft's official site for learning Visual Basic, which is a popular language for website developers:

http://msdn.microsoft.com/en-us/vbasic/ms789192.aspx

The following is Microsoft's official site for learning C# and .NET development; these tools are the accepted method for developing large desktop applications for the PC.

http://msdn.microsoft.com/en-us/vcsharp/default.aspx

Web Development

The following site will educate you on PHP, which is a popular web-based language. Most WordPress blogs use PHP, and this information could get you started in a rapidly growing industry:

http://devzone.zend.com/article/627

The following is a PHP site that covers more material than the "beginner's" sites:

http://www.w3schools.com/PHP/DEfaULT.asP

The following site will educate you on ASP (Active Server Pages), which is a popular web-based language. Similar to PHP, knowledge of ASP pages is nearly mandatory if you plan to do sophisticated web page work:

http://www.w3schools.com/asp/default.asp

Answers to exercises

Chapter 1: Evolution of software

1. A switch is either "on" or "off," which is equivalent to "1" or "0."

2. 100

3. 1001

4. 100

5. Very large numbers can be represented with less digits than using binary.

Chapter 2: Anatomy of processing

Disk drive – Peripheral
RAM – Memory
Computer speed – Clock
Accesses memory – Processor
Keyboard – Peripheral
Data storage – Memory
Execution of program – Processor
Fed instructions – Processor
Computer heartbeat – Clock

Chapter 3: The evolution of computer language

1. A program is written in text symbols and words that a computer processor does not understand. It therefore needs to be translated into codes that can be understood by the computer.

2. Each processor instruction can be represented by an "English" text symbol. This is easier for humans to read, but these symbols are translated into native machine codes.

3. If machine codes were entered directly into a computer, inserting new codes in the middle would move subsequent locations, making all branch locations invalid.

4. Computer languages are for people, not for machines. The language is translated into machine codes before it is executed.

Chapter 4: Introduction to C

1. A semicolon terminates a statement. Without a semicolon, the compilers assumes the next line is part of the same statement.

2. A variable is a placeholder that contains a value. A pointer "points" to a variable, and is designated by a "*" character

3. An array of 16 integers is being declared. Each separate integer can be accessed with brackets, as array[0], array[1], array[2], etc.

4. An operator assigns a value to a variable, or compares another value to a variable. An example of an operator would be "=" (one variable = another value).

5. A conditional operator performs a comparison of two variables or a variable and a value. Examples:

   ```
   x > y // x is greater than y
   x == 0 // x equals 0
   ```

6. Curly braces define a block of code. One use for such a block is a set of statements following a comparison:

   ```
   if (x > 0)
   {
   statement...
   statement...
   }
   ```

7. A function is a block of code that performs a specific task. A program consists of many functions. An example of a function might be a set of statements to determine what day of the week corresponds to a given month, day, and year.

8. A local variable is defined inside a function, in which case, only statements within the function can reference the variable. A global variable is defined outside a function and can be referenced by any statement in any function.

Chapter 6: Hands-on for Windows

1. The loop is infinite. It needs a "break" statement to end.

2.
```
int  x = 0;
while (x < 8)
{
x = x + 1;
}
```

3. Using many "if-then-else" statements can be stated in much simpler terms, and less code, using a "switch" statement.

4. You would usually define a new type to identify it more clearly in a program. For example, "typedef int accountNumber" defines "accountNumber" to be the same as an int, but its usage is more clear when referenced later in the program.

5. Using a macro to define a specific value allows you to use that macro name throughout the program. If you needed to modify the value, you only need to change one place. For example, if "offsetToName" was equivalent to the value 22, you could change it to 23 and subsequently, all occurrences of "offsetToName" throughout your program would be changed to the new value.

6. A struct "groups" multiple variables together into a single "package." For example, if several variables are inside a struct, you only need to pass one item (instead of several) to a function.

7.
```
typedef sruct{
int anInt;
double aDoubleValue;
char someString[2];
} myStruct;
```

Chapter 9: Introduction to C++

1. A C++ class can have functions, including a constructor and destructor function that get called automatically when the class is instantiated.

2. A class definition is merely a definition, or a "template." To instantiate a class means it becomes a usable data structure that is live in your program.

3. One: To declare a variable of the class type. Two: To create an instance using "new."

4. The constructor function is called automatically when the class is instantiated. The constructor is used to initialize data elements inside the class.

5. Going "out of scope" means that the instance will no longer be used or referenced. An instance goes out of scope either when it was declared inside a code block and that block has terminated, or when "delete" is used.

6. The compiler matches the function that contains the data types you are passing to the function parameters.

7. An inherited class means that all definitions of the class being inherited are included in the new class.

Glossary

C++ An extension of C. See class.

application A software program that runs independently of other programs and performs specific task(s).

argument A value passed to a function. This is used interchangeably with parameter.

array A series of elements that can be indexed individually.

assembly (language) The native language of a computer processor. Each machine instruction is represented by an "English" word or syllable.

binary A base-2 numbering system in which each digit of a number is represented by a "0" or "1." Binary is a computer's native numbering system.

body The part of a function that executes, as opposed to its declaration. The body portion lies between curly braces.

C A computer language that has become the language of choice for modern programming.

cast A method to inform a compiler to treat a variable as another type. Hence, (int)x will cast "x" as an integer regardless of what type "x" might be. Sometimes used interchangeably with coerce.

class A group of functions and variables that act as a single unit, or object. The class is an integral part of C++.

clock An oscillator in computer hardware that steps a processor through its program and provides timing for peripherals. A clock is said to be the heartbeat of a computer.

code Literally, a binary code that is interpreted by a processor to perform a low-level task. Today, "code" has come to mean any software development, as in, "This program is a lot of code.".

coerce A method to "force" one type of variable to a different type. See cast.

compiler A program that translates textual statements into machine-readable codes in order for the processor to execute the program.

conditional statement A condition for the processor to execute an instruction. The condition is based on the comparison of two variables. Example: "if X > Y, then do something.".

constructor A function within a C++ class that gets automatically called when the class if first instantiated. See instance.

destructor A function within a C++ class that gets automatically called when the class is being deleted or has gone out of scope.

for-loop A programming loop that begins with a "for" statement.

function A block of code that executes a specific task, and optionally returns a value to the caller of the function.

gig (gigabyte) Approximately 1 billion bytes.

global (variable) A variable that is accessible to any part of an entire program, as opposed to a local variable that is accessible only within the code block where it exists.

header (file) A file that contains definitions of functions that are implemented elsewhere.

hex (hexadecimal) A base-16 numbering system. Hexadecimal is used frequently to represent larger, binary numbers. A hexadecimal digit is represented with 0-9, then A, B, C, D and F to make 16 possible values.

implementation The part of a function that contains the actual programming instructions. See prototype.

inheritance A C++ class that is based on some other class. It is said to inherit all the attributes of the "parent" class.

instance The creation of a C++ class or pointer to a class. Until there is an instance of a class, it is only a definition but not implemented.

iOS The operating system for Apple "i" products (iPod, iPhone, iPad, etc.).

K (kilobyte) Approxmately 1,000 bytes. Technically, a kilobyte is 1024 bytes.

loop A block of code that continues to repeat until a specific conditions is met.

macro A variable or block of code that is substituted for a single symbol. A macro definition always begins with the keyword #define.

memory Data storage in a computer. Memory can be accessed by the processor and by other peripherals.

object An entity created by a program that contains functions and variables. An object acts as a "group." Also called a class in C++.

Objective-C A C-like language used in the Mac OS environment..

operator A notation that defines the relationship between two variables. For example, an equal sign ("=") is an operator, as in X = Y.

OS-X The operating system for the Apple Macintosh.

overloading The act of defining two or more functions with the same name, but with different function arguments. The compiler decides which function to call based on the type of data being passed to the function. Overloading is legal only in C++.

overriding The act of defining the same function in a subclass as in its parent class, and the parent class function is defined as "virtual." If so, the subclass function is said to override the parent when the function is called at runtime.

parameter A value passed to a function. Used interchangeably with argument.

peripheral Any external device controlled by the computer. Examples of peripherals would be printers, modems, and disk drives.

pointer An address to a memory allocation. Pointers in C are represented with the * symbol (a *char is a pointer to a character or characters).

processor The device inside a computer that executes all programs.

program, programming A series of steps and tasks to be executed by a computer processor.

prototype (function) A function declaration that does not yet have a body, but is declared so the compiler knows the full function exists elsewhere.

RAM Abbreviation for Random Access Memory. This is computer data storage in which any one of its locations can be instantly accessed by the processor.

scope The area where a variable or class instance "lives." A variable or class in C is said to be in scope as long as it is inside curly braces.

source, source code The original, textual file that was written by the programmer. Native processors do not understand source code, and hence, a compiler is required to translate source code into machine-readable code.

string A series of characters. "This is a string" would be an example.

struct, structure A definition in C that contains a list of variables as a group.

subclass A C++ class that is based on another class. When a subclass is defined, it assumes all the characteristics of the original class.

switch statement A list of code blocks, each of which get executed based on some specific condition.

typedef A keyword to define a new variable type that is based on an existing type. Example: "typedef int myInt" tells a compiler that "myInt" is a new, additonal name for the type "int.".

variable A symbol or word that contains a value inside a program. A variable can be one of many types, including an integer, a fraction, or a character array.

virtual A keyword in C++ that tells the compiler that a subclass can have the same function as the parent class. At runtime, the subclass function is called instead of the parent function, which is known as overriding.

while-loop A programming loop that begins or ends with "while." While a condition remains true, the loop continues.

Xcode The development system for Apple Macintosh and Apple devices.

Index